The Political Crisis
of
the Enterprise System

D1292665

THE POLITICAL CRISIS
OF
THE ENTERPRISE SYSTEM

Richard Eells

Studies of the Modern Corporation
Graduate School of Business
Columbia University

MACMILLAN PUBLISHING CO., INC.
NEW YORK

Collier Macmillan Publishers
LONDON

338.973   R26p
c-1

Copyright © 1980 by the Trustees of Columbia University
in the City of New York

All rights reserved. No part of this book may be reproduced or
transmitted in any form or by any means, electronic or mechanical,
including photocopying, recording, or by any information storage and
retrieval system, without permission in writing from the Publisher.

Macmillan Publishing Co., Inc.
866 Third Avenue, New York, N.Y. 10022

Collier Macmillan Canada, Ltd.

Library of Congress Catalog Card Number: 79–48016

Printed in the United States of America

printing number

1 2 3 4 5 6 7 8 9 10

Library of Congress Cataloging in Publication Data

Eells, Richard Sedric Fox
    The political crisis of the enterprise system.

    (Studies of the modern corporation)
    Includes index.
    1. Industry and state—United States. 2. Industry
—Social aspects—United States. 3. Business and poli-
tics—United States. 4. Industry and state.
I. Title. II. Series.
HD3616.U46E33 1980   338.973   79-48016
ISBN 0-02-909250-7

Books by Richard Eells

Corporation Giving in a Free Society

The Meaning of Modern Business

Conceptual Foundations of Business
(with Clarence Walton)

The Government of Corporations

*The Business System: Readings in
Ideas and Concepts*, 3 vols.
(ed. with Clarence Walton)

The Corporation and the Arts

Education and the Business Dollar
(with Kenneth G. Patrick)

Man in the City of the Future
(ed. with Clarence Walton)

*Global Corporations: The Emerging System of
World Economic Power*

Bribery and Extortion in World Business
(with Neil H. Jacoby and Peter Nehemkis)

International Business Philanthropy
(editor)

The Political Crisis of the Enterprise System

STUDIES OF THE MODERN CORPORATION
Graduate School of Business, Columbia University

The Program for Studies of the Modern Corporation is devoted to the advancement and dissemination of knowledge about the corporation. Its publications are designed to stimulate inquiry, research, criticism, and reflection. They fall into three categories: works by outstanding businessmen, scholars, and professional men from a variety of backgrounds and academic disciplines; annotated and edited selections of business literature; and business classics that merit republication. The studies are supported by outside grants from private business, professional, and philanthropic institutions interested in the program's objectives.

This book is dedicated to
the memory of my friend and colleague
Neil H. Jacoby
1909–1979

Contents

Contents

Contents

Preface

THE central theme of this book is the survival of the enterprise system during the next fifty years. In pursuing that goal I believe corporations must maximize the contribution they can make to solve the many problems our world faces. To do this they must take the time and thought to develop clear positions on the critical public policy issues of our day—and make them known.

The evolving role of the large business corporation as one of the major actors on the world stage is certainly one of the most fascinating subjects of the present era. That role includes not just considerations of the effectiveness of business as an economic instrument of profit and growth, but also questions of the wider sociological, psychological, ethical, and political significance of the workplace of so many millions of modern people. The philosophical issues of the human potential of the business corporation as well as the value of the enterprise system to our society generally are likewise included.

This short book, which precedes a longer study, is an attempt to diagnose what looms more and more as the severe political crisis of the private enterprise system and to prescribe a few strategies to improve its prospects for the future. In all the problems examined here the root problem of business, the corporation, and the enterprise system is political. The private economic sector, despite its access to enormous resources, seems curiously help-less when it comes to protecting itself in the political arena. The steady encroachment of regulation, the high corporate taxation rate, the public criticism of business by political leaders, the poor hearing that business gets in the media—all are essentially political problems. And the solution to these problems that the public apparently contemplates is more and more management of the economic sector by government bureaucracies.

Many of the themes articulated here—looking at the internal structure and external relations of the large corporation in terms of political theory; corporate governance; business philanthropy; business intelligence—have been areas of my own professional interests. In fact, each of these has been the subject of earlier books, essays, or lectures. These areas have developed over several decades, and their importance and urgency continues to increase, I believe, in our current global setting.

Many corporate leaders today endorse these views, although there still are those who believe that corporate leadership is ill-advised to attend to the social and political environment, and even more ill-advised to think of the corporation as playing an active role in shaping our society. These voices cling to the belief that any attention to these matters detracts from performance and profitability. Still others believe it is harmful for business to acknowledge openly and strongly the wastefulness and inefficiency of certain forms of government regulation, fearing that such directness will inadvertently fuel anti-business sentiment. That approach runs the risk, I fear, of inviting a new wave of demands for government regulation. It is better, I believe, to address squarely the fundamental issues of our society than to wait until the charges of corporate irresponsibility reach a crescendo.

The insights of a number of people have been particularly helpful in the writing of this book. I am most deeply grateful to the late Dr. Neil H. Jacoby, the founding Dean of the UCLA Graduate School of Management and a close friend for many years, with whom I discussed many of the themes of this book.

In addition, I had useful conversations about the ideas presented here with: Dr. Graham T. Allison, Jr., Dean, John F. Kennedy School of Government, Harvard University; Professor Robert O. Carlson, Executive Dean, Schools of Business, Adelphi University; Dr. Giulio Pontecorvo, Professor of Business, Graduate School of Business, Columbia University; Dr. Leonard R. Sayles, Professor of Business, Graduate School of Business, Columbia University; A. A. Sommer, Jr., Esq., former Commissioner, Securities and Exchange Commission; Dr. George A. Steiner, Harry and Elsa Kunin Professor of Business and Society, Graduate School of Management, UCLA; Judge Herbert A. Stern, U.S. District Court for the District of New Jersey; Gus Tyler, Assistant President, International Ladies Garment Workers Union; Dr. J. Fred Weston, Professor of Business, Graduate School of Management, UCLA; and Dr. Harvey Wheeler, political scientist. Finally I wish to acknowledge with gratitude the application of research skills and insights to Steven E. Halliwell.

RICHARD EELLS
New York City
January, 1980

Introduction

As the twentieth century comes to a close, private enterprise is under pervasive attack, and its continued existence is in doubt. Throughout the world, the private sector is steadily receding in the face of mounting control by
the public (governmental) sector. There are instances
where current prospects for private business are encouraging, but these situations are the exceptions.

The reasons for this steady increase in governmental
power are themselves complex and deeply rooted. In socialist countries, of course, government has long substituted for the private initiative of the entrepreneurial
class. Most Third World nations, lacking many of the social forces that brought about the enterprise system in
the West, tend to substitute government structures for
market mechanisms. But even in the advanced industrial states, where private enterprise has been the instrument for the achievement of unparalleled economic
growth, the tendency toward giving increased prerogatives to the public sector has continued unabated for
many years.

The attack on the private enterprise system* reflects a

---

* Throughout this book, the terms "the private enterprise system" or simply,
"the enterprise system" are used in preference to "capitalism" or the "capitalist order" because they emphasize the socio-political dimensions of this economic order. The term "capitalism," in contrast, applied to a country, defines
primarily its economic order. Only in the discussion of ideological issues—the

deep crisis in Western civilization. It is, in fact, a crisis for the survival of the system of private associations of which the business corporation is a major component. The crisis can be thought of in another way, namely, as reflecting the decline of the private social and economic institutions on which our value system is built and through which most of our daily lives are experienced. It is that wide range of activity, which has taken place outside the purview or supervision of public government, that has vitalized our culture and permitted private enterprise to assume a central role in industrial development throughout the world. If the current attacks on private enterprise were but one more round of government encroachment on business, it would be cause for the most serious concern. But these attacks have now reached the point that we must ask a question that goes beyond the immediate question of government-business relations: how will this steady erosion of private initiative that has accompanied the assault on private enterprise affect the political and social order under which the West has flourished?

Ultimately, the question of government control over private enterprise is intimately tied to the fate of the rights of the individual and the political freedoms on which our political system is based. A historic tradition now extending back some 500 years—and even further, in embryonic form—has welded freedom from arbitrary acts of government with the right of private economic activity. Without a system of private associations to counterbalance the powers of public government, the society is threatened by the same bureaucratic and authoritarian

---

conflicts with socialist movements, for example—is the analysis couched in terms of "capitalism." It should be understood, however, that the various terms, as used in this text, refer to the same phenomenon.

strangulation that we see in many places around the world.

Thus, the attack on private enterprise presents a fundamental challenge to the political and human rights that form the cornerstone of political and social reality in the West. Recognizing this, we do not mean to imply that all those who turn toward government for remedies to the complex problems of our age are advocates of ultimate totalitarian rule. Indeed, it is evident that government has a key role to play in certain aspects of any viable future social order; the unprecedented level of global interdependence that we have now achieved makes certain aspects of social planning a necessity. But those who favor ever-increasing government control need to be more conscious of the dangers implicit in all-encompassing government.

The challenge rightly falls to the leaders of large business corporations, who must now rethink the strategies for maintaining the well-being of the various elements of the private sector, on which the strength and vitality of the enterprise system depend. The large corporation cannot become a substitute for inherent governmental functions. What the executive leadership of the business community can do, on the one hand, is to design steps to strengthen the private sector, and, on the other hand, to maintain a momentum of profitability and growth. In alliance with leaders of other key segments of the private sector—universities, foundations, religious and professional organizations, labor unions, and private policy research groups—the business community must work to preserve the essential values of this culture by meeting the challenge of the present crisis. It is a difficult and most awesome responsibility, but the future of our political and economic order rests on its success. The alternative is to watch the gradual—and seemingly inexorable —accretion of government power continue, and the scope of the private sector gradually diminish, until the last vestige of individual freedom and the concept of the private association has been eliminated.

In the pages that follow, this book will consider the future of the large corporation, the problems it confronts (both now and in the future), and how it can act to protect itself and the private enterprise system of which it is an integral element.

1

The Nature of the Attack

The Global Attack

To understand the American private enterprise system, and the depth of the attack upon it, it is necessary to approach the problem from a global as well as a domestic point of view. The enterprise system operates on a global basis, joining together firms and individuals from far distant places in the search for new markets, new products, and new profits. In the widest sense, the enterprise system is a set of voluntary associations directed at the fulfillment of the aspiration for economic survival and increased profits. It is in this aspiration, this fundamental drive or impulse, that the smallest shopkeeper and the greatest multinational combines can be seen as part of a common system. Moving beyond such fundamentals, the system immediately becomes complex: major organizational adaptations occur as firms grow and refine the various procedures—production, marketing, finance, planning—by which their profitability is maintained or

1

enhanced. In brief, the core impulse remains unaltered, but the instrumentalities of successful entrepreneurship shift dramatically as we consider firms of greater size.

The large multinational corporation represents the most advanced adaptation of basic enterprise principles and, for the analyst, the greatest conceptual challenge. Going beyond the relatively secure environment of national institutions within which it was founded and developed, the private multinational corporation establishes various economic ties—commercial, financial, investment—in foreign settings. In ways that reflect the particular firm's market setting and basic production requisites, the multinational firm integrates these foreign relationships into its overall operations.

Through this extension of enterprise activity abroad, the private enterprise system has created a global network of economic as well as political ties that cut across the various national lines. Major global markets—the U.S. and the countries of Western Europe—now draw on production facilities throughout the world and, at the same time, transfer to those centers the goods, resources, and skills that our advanced economic order can provide. The basic structure through which all of these transactions occur is the enterprise system—agreements between individuals or business corporations, which each participant regards as advantageous and profitable. Even in the socialist states, where most economic activity is centrally planned by government agencies, private firms from the enterprise-oriented countries conduct business through contractual arrangements with those regimes.

This impressive spread of enterprise activity around the globe has not, however, been without a concomitant increase in risks. As this system has expanded, spurred by the motive of personal and corporate gain for all involved, it has transformed itself and the societies in which it has become implanted. Reaction to these changes has ranged from welcome and acceptance (by those who understand and appreciate the system's potential benefits) to armed attack (by opposition elements of the most extreme variety).

Corporations of the size that bridge oceans comfortably are heavily reliant on stable and predictable environments for successful operation; it is no wonder that roughly three-quarters of all U.S. overseas investment is in Western Europe, where the economic climate is most easily appraised by U.S. businessmen. Transfer of enterprise methodology into less-developed areas of the world faces the attendant financial risks of inadequate communications, transportation, and distribution systems. It also faces the jeopardy imposed by the political instability of people whose poverty makes the well-organized and well-financed operations of a foreign corporation an irresistible target.

An accurate assessment of the global attack on the enterprise system, then, must begin with a recognition of the diverse ways in which this system is threatened. Some of the most significant ways in which the enterprise system is under attack are:

- *Electoral Takeovers:* In various parts of the world—Western Europe, most notably—socialist and communist parties are making strong bids for control of governments. Their accession to power enhances the prospects of nationalization with little likelihood of adequate compensation.
- *Guerrilla Wars:* Throughout the developing world, movements of various nationalist, separatist, and ideological coloration are conducting armed warfare and disrupting local economic opportunities.
- *International Cartels:* Cartelization of the international trade in petroleum by OPEC has disturbed the patterns of production, international credit flows, and the future in-

3

vestment plans of the private enterprise petroleum companies, which constitute a central part of the enterprise system.
- *Government Regulation:* International bodies and national governments continually increase the number of controls of private economic activity and stretch the frontiers of regulation to apply to new aspects of corporate action.
- *Terrorism:* Business executives as well as political leaders have become increasingly subject to assassination attempts and kidnappings.[1]

This list is not exhaustive. And activities inimical to the interests of the enterprise system do not come only from self-proclaimed political opponents—nor do they remain constant. On the other hand, it should not be assumed that every disruptive event in world politics is a threat to the enterprise system, nor that every foe is a permanent adversary. It should not go unnoticed, for example, that the most encouraging prospect for new large-scale enterprise activity at the present time is an avowedly anti-capitalist regime—the People's Republic of China. Some analysts not unsympathetic to enterprise economics will argue that guerilla opposition to politically and socially backward regimes is likely to improve conditions and opportunities for large corporations in the foreseeable future by forcing reforms that will moderate and stabilize these societies. Thus, deciphering the nature of threats to the enterprise system is an increasingly subtle craft and not one reducible to simple sloganeering.

The general drift of global events should not be lost sight of, however, because of interesting specific cases. The assault on the enterprise system is great, and it is growing on many fronts. Current worldwide trends toward government expansion could, if allowed to continue unabated, bring about the dismantling of this vital and integrative mode of economic activity as early as the end

4

of this century. The major accomplishments of the enterprise system as the engine of economic development should not be permitted to conceal the enormous risks and vulnerabilities that have developed.

The world enterprise system, like any vital organism, is dynamic. It will not survive while another generation finds its bearings: either the enterprise system must regain its firm footing and re-establish an appropriate balance with political forces or it will continue to slip toward instability and a system of government regulation of all the vital aspects of society.

The Attack in the Industrial States

Nowhere is the crisis more advanced than among the industrial states of Western Europe, where socialists are on the verge—despite some recent reverses—of taking over governments through electoral victories in several nations. The threat to the global enterprise system of such a shift is great: Europe is second only to the United States as the heartland of the enterprise system and the values on which it rests. Western Europe is the cradle of capitalism, and the birthplace of the great philosophical and moral concepts that have shaped our theories as well as our practice of government. On a pragmatic level, a major shift of political allegiance would drastically disturb international relations. Thus, there is much at stake in Western Europe which, since World War II, has coexisted uneasily with a set of socialist governments on its Eastern frontier. The presence of Soviet troops throughout Eastern Europe has provided a constant reminder of the vulnerability of Western Europe to military attack, and has shaped the political atmosphere as well. Deep divisions and a strong socialist movement are not new to Western Europe, but the strategic consequences of their growth in power have changed significantly in the post-war period.

Eurocommunism

The most striking recent development in this evolving situation is the emergence of the Eurocommunist movement. In the past, communist parties in Western Europe adhered very strictly to the pronouncements from Moscow regarding every aspect of communist theory and practice. This strategy was followed in the name of "socialist internationalism," a doctrine that argued that the greatest advances for socialism—and eventually, communism—internationally would be accomplished by a unified front of the world's communist forces. Moscow's party, as the ruling power of the first socialist regime, claimed the authority to dictate what "line" all other parties were to follow.

But then there was the Yugoslavian break. And, in 1960, the unified front dissolved with the Chinese communist regime's break from Moscow. European communist parties, however, maintained orthodox communist positions. By the mid-1970s the European communist movement began to take official stands that suggested the development of diversity within the world communist movement. Each country, it was said, must find its own "road to socialism," implying that Moscow's judgment was not necessarily the best. In a further move of seeming significance, European communists dropped "the dictatorship of the proletariat," a key Marxist doctrine, from their theoretical vocabulary. It seemed as if the communists were moving into a more moderate posture and seeking to shed their image as "agents of Moscow."

Soviet human rights policies also provided an impetus

for the European parties to disassociate themselves. Trials of Soviet dissidents were a constant source of embarrassment to them, and the European parties pledged to accept a pluralistic political system and agreed to "develop all individual and collective freedoms." Throughout the postwar era, communists throughout Europe have found it useful or necessary to take an expansive, open posture toward national issues and other political parties on various occasions. But such announcements of moderation and independence have been viewed with scepticism by many communist-watchers.

In a recent analysis of Eurocommunism, Henry Kissinger cited numerous cases of East European communist leadership proclaiming, in the immediate postwar era, support for parliamentary democracy, a multi-party system, and strict allegiance to democratically oriented constitutions. In each case, however, these pronouncements were soon followed by seizures of absolute power and the nationalization of all private industries. The new-found liberalism of the European communists, Kissinger argues, is not really very new.

> I find it hard to believe that after decades of vilifying Social Democracy and treating it as their mortal enemy, especially in every Communist country, Communist parties have suddenly become Social Democrats. Whether or not they are independent of Moscow, Communists represent a philosophy which by its very nature and their own testimony stands outside the "bourgeois" framework of Western constitutional history.[2]

In recent months, Kissinger's doubts have been confirmed. At the 23rd Congress of the French Communist Party, held early in 1979, dissident elements that had questioned Soviet human rights policies were noticeably

7

absent, and the high-level Soviet delegation was warmly greeted as the Congress returned to the traditional call for "international solidarity," a signal of Moscow's pre-eminence.

So it can be seen that the tendency toward independence, which had been hailed as a major breakthrough in the political deadlock that grips Europe, has proven to be chimerical. In France and Italy, and to a lesser degree in Spain, communists have a large enough bloc of voter support to pose a continuing threat to political and economic stability. A communist entry into the governments of these countries will undoubtedly lead to new and more stringent controls on the rights of private ownership, the movement of capital, and the levels of permissible profits. Nationalization of new sectors of the economy are likely, as are confiscatory taxes, which will nullify any investor incentive.

The investment climate has already been seriously dampened by the prospect of a socialist-communist electoral victory. Given the uncertainty of future conditions, a great deal of European wealth is leaving the continent. It is now commonplace to find Europeans buying farmland in Vermont, condominiums in Miami, or cooperative apartments in New York. Rising property values in the U.S. may make such investments a wise choice, but it is evident that there is more than monetary gain involved in the decision—Europe's wealthier strata are losing confidence in the future of their countries.

There is an additional gloomy aspect to the current picture in Western Europe: its economic recovery after World War II was closely tied to the presence—economic, diplomatic, and military—of the United States on the continent. By its presence, the United States has helped foster some foundation for an integrated European economic and governmental structure. For Americans, a renewed Europe with a vigorous economic base was a bulwark against Soviet encroachment; for the Europeans themselves, a unified politico-economic structure provided some basis for an independent stance toward the United States as well as toward the Soviets and their allies. A government led by a socialist-communist alliance in any of these countries, however, would not be likely to respect the strategic rationale that has allowed so much economic progress. Even a regime independent of Moscow would probably not be enthusiastic about maintaining the defense, commercial, and financial arrangements that have given the Atlantic Alliance its vitality over the past thirty years. Thus, a shift in a single European government could throw the entire continent's economic activity into serious disorder.

Despite this pessimistic outlook, there is still little sense of impending crisis among U.S. business leaders. Perhaps they are preoccupied with other matters, or perhaps they are doubtful that the people of France, Italy, or Spain would ever actually vote the communists into power. There is some validity to the argument that the communists would be reluctant to take responsibility for an economy with all the problems that currently face Europe—it would reflect badly on their philosophy if they were unable to eradicate those problems easily. (Marxists are historically much more successful, it should be noted, as critics and revolutionaries than they are as managers of complex societies.)

But such views, were the communist leadership to adopt them, would only confirm their confidence that the crisis can only grow deeper. Increased government intervention in the private sector by non-socialist leaders would serve merely to smooth the transition to a full take-over of economic activity by the state under future socialist regimes.

Britain and the Commonwealth

The victory of Margaret Thatcher in the spring of 1979 suggests to some that the British population has begun to move away from the government-oriented politics that have dominated its evolution for the past fifteen years.

The problems that Britain faces, however, have a long lineage and deep causes. The wartime devastation of Britain and the subsequent loss of her imperial possessions forced a serious contraction in British economic strength, as reflected by long-term inflationary pressures and the devaluation of the pound. Even the flow of North Sea oil has not provided a significant reprieve from the constant pressures the British economy has faced in the postwar era.

Government regulation has been substituted in a number of areas for private initiative in the British ordeal, including the on-again/off-again nationalization of several significant industrial sectors. Social pressures for big government have also been increased by migrations of Indians and people from the West Indies to London. These immigrants, seeking to escape dismal economic conditions at home, have become a threat to the status and employment of lower-income white Londoners, and violent street battles have occurred. As a consequence, economic pressures for expanded government are augmented by social unrest.

Thus, the Thatcher cabinet faces a set of problems that may not be responsive to traditional Conservative Party remedies. The impulse to revive the ailing private sector by loosening restraints may be legitimate, but it is not clear that it will be sufficient. Years of high taxation, nationalizations, and growing social instability may have weakened the private sector too greatly to expect a spontaneous recovery once some of the burdens have been lifted.

The Commonwealth states do not provide a much rosier picture. Canada, despite its abundant resources, has suffered serious currency devaluations, trade imbalances, and unemployment over the past several years. The threat of Quebec separation seems to have immobilized the entire national economy, and Quebec's problems show no signs of early resolution. Australia seems forever gripped in serious problems with its Labour Party; South Africa and Rhodesia, beset by racial issues they seem incapable of resolving, are not promising arenas for private initiative in the foreseeable future. And India has moved in recent years even farther away from private investment and toward state control than it had in the decades since independence.

Germany and Japan

Two of the vanquished powers of World War II, Germany and Japan, are, ironically, the most vigorous of the postwar economies. One wonders if being spared the debilitating military expenses of the Cold War was central to the economic accomplishments that have marked each of these states. For whatever reasons, each of these economies has proven itself capable of long-term expansion led by trade surpluses that have given their respective currencies an admirable stability in recent years.

However, both economies are quite vulnerable to changes in the world economic climate. Japan, with a virtual total dependence on imported energy, can only continue its economic expansion if world markets are healthy and energy supplies available at reasonable costs. Germany's central bank is predicting level future growth, and some fundamental restructuring is seen as essential for future expansion, as pressure on less sophisticated industries grows from cheaper Third World labor.

It also should be noted that these two countries have spawned two of the fiercest and most dangerous terrorist organizations of the modern era, which may prove to be a symptom of deep internal problems for these relatively healthy economies. Japan's Red Army and Germany's Baader-Meinhof Gang have significantly affected the international climate, and provoked a spiraling increase in national and corporate security forces. Governments of both these states have equated economic strength with recovery of national pride and thus tended to leave unresolved issues of responsibility for the war. If the high incidence of terrorism in Germany and Japan does reflect some deep-rooted sources of political controversy, it is likely that these countries will show symptoms of recurrent political instability for the indefinite future.

The Attack in the Developing World

During the Cold War era, government leaders in some of the poorer nations—led by India's Nehru—began to identify themselves as separate from the two great protagonists of that conflict, the United States and Russia. Calling themselves "non-aligned" to indicate their unwillingness to stand with either side, this amalgamation of underdeveloped states gradually became known as the "Third World"—not the free enterprise world, not the communist world, but something else.

In spite of two decades of conferences, published analyses, and confrontations within the group, the Third World is still a confusing and contradiction-ridden entity. In the United Nations, where a significant part of the political energy of the Third World is focused, the Third World caucus (known as the Group of 77, to indicate the original size of its membership—there are now well over 100 states included) brings together nations of every conceivable kind: right-wing military regimes; left-wing religious governments; states with gigantic populations; states with less than a million citizens. Recently, the Rumanian government decided to join the Group, an indication of its independence from the Soviet Union and an acknowledgement of its low level of economic development. Adding an Eastern bloc nation to the Group will hardly bring new clarity to the struggle for purpose and direction, however.

Various research centers throughout the world that monitor global trends regularly bombard us with dizzying statistics on the wretched conditions that prevail in the underdeveloped countries and the likelihood of even greater catastrophe in the near future. In the midst of these sordid conditions, military clashes are frequent, governments change hands often, and corruption is widespread. Separatist movements seem to arise whenever authoritarian rule is reduced, and much of the energy of each government seems to be devoted to justifying, protecting, and reinforcing its control over a largely illiterate and malnourished population.

For the leadership of large business corporations, conducting business in this setting can be a very difficult and highly risky process. Questionable financial and accounting methods, hostile political forces, and takeover attempts have made firms less than enthusiastic about investing in Third World countries. Cultural patterns that differ markedly from traditional Western ones—different views of time, family ties, social propriety, and even the distance at which individuals converse—add further cause for reticence. Nonetheless, the underdeveloped world is rich in resources sought by the advanced countries; in addition, the cheap labor available in these poorer countries is an increasingly important component in the functioning of the advanced economies as technological improvements continue to demand an upgrading of their labor forces at home.

What does all this mean for the enterprise system as a global force? The socialist rhetoric of some regimes suggests a strong aversion to private investment, though often their economic policies belie their rhetoric. Far more significantly, the development of the enterprise system is hindered by the endemic disorder of the Third World regions of the globe. Their continued instability, fragmentation, and military conflict delay indefinitely the time when the rational and integrated development of markets and resources by the advanced economic organizations of the multinational firm could come to the aid of the huge proportion of the Third World's people who live in these intolerable conditions. And each day that passes increases the dependence of these nations on governmental structures of the most authoritarian kind.

Sub-Saharan Africa

Africa provides perhaps the best example of the seemingly impenetrable problems the enterprise system faces in the Third World. Each major region—West, East, Central and Southern—is the scene of serious instability. In the West, Nigeria is attempting to move toward parliamentary rule after more than a decade of military coups and countercoups: its prospects are limited, however, by strong regionalism, pervasive governmental corruption, and a lack of coherent development plans. Nigeria, one of the largest foreign suppliers of U.S. oil, is the key to the entire region, given its natural resources and large population. Yet ships regularly stand in the harbor off Lagos for weeks waiting to off-load, traffic congestion in

the capital is intolerable, and communications highly un-
reliable. The recent coup in nearby Ghana, another state
supposedly returning to elected rule after years of military government, certainly does not help. East Africa is a
virtual armed camp as Ethiopian, Eritrean, and Somali
forces battle for terrain whose proximity to the Mideast
oil shipping lanes gives it strategic import.

The Central region recently witnessed the collapse of
three dictatorships that have caused great suffering and
dislocation for years; in the South, the "front-line states"
live in a state of perpetual siege as the racial conflict in
Rhodesia/Zimbabwe and South Africa continues to boil.
The most important survival action of the enterprise system on the entire continent in recent years was Gulf Oil's
successful retention of production in Angola's Cabinda
oilfields as the ruling power shifted from Portugal to the
new socialist regime. In one of the ironies that punctuate
our times, the perimeters of the Gulf facility are report-
edly protected by Cuban forces.

Latin America and South America

The brightest places for enterprise economics in the
southern two-thirds of the Western hemisphere are Brazil
and Mexico. Both of these states have carved out places
as industrializing nations in the developing world, their
growth fueled by abundant natural resources, particularly oil and gas in Mexico. Each economy, however, operates with restrictions on the entry of private capital
from abroad, thus limiting the terms on which they will
become integrated into a global system. Furthermore,
both regimes are subject to strong oppositional forces
from within: dissatisfaction with the political censorship
of the Brazilian generals has kept political dissent sim-
mering in the major cities, and Mexican President Lopez

15

Portillo is furthering his development strategy amidst a set of political animosities that have traditionally held back Mexican economic progress.

For each of these states, the dark clouds of population pressure overshadow long-term economic prospects. Sao Paulo and Mexico City, according to demographic projections, will have populations of 12.5 million early in the 21st century, which will result in an inconceivably high level of pressure on urban services that are already over-taxed. Between six and seven hundred thousand Mexicans enter the job market each year, and unemployment stands at roughly 25 percent. Even with the most optimistic growth projections, Mexico would be hard-pressed to meet the demands for new jobs as its population continues to grow.

Thus, even in the most promising centers of Latin America and South America, the options for the enterprise system are limited, due to the population explosion. International population specialists are fond of pointing out that "development is the best contraceptive," but it is not clear that the large firms of the industrial states will be permitted to meet the challenge.

In the rest of Latin and South America, it is extremely difficult to be optimistic. Guerrilla raids and socialist rhetoric clash with military regimes loyal to quasi-feudal elites, making real economic initiative impractical. It is impossible to predict the direction of the new Nicaraguan regime, and its long-term effects on the stability of the region.

The Islamic World

The overthrow of the Shah of Iran disrupted world petroleum markets and underscored the tenuous relationship that U.S. and other foreign investments have in nations with the serious social dislocations associated with economic underdevelopment. Throughout the Arab and other Islamic states stretching from Senegal and Morocco on the Atlantic coast of Africa to Indonesia in the Southern Pacific, opposition to the social transformations associated with economic change is putting severe pressures on foreign investors. Much of the discontent is channeled through the traditional vehicle of Islam, with the result that all outside values or involvements are suspect. Corruption is widespread in many of these states, and enterprise methods are tarred with the same brush that is used to attack the local rulers. Instability throughout this region is likely to increase as the example of Iran is pursued by would-be reformers and revolutionaries in each country.

Asian Export Centers

The gradual upgrading of the technological base of the huge Japanese export industry has prompted the development throughout Asia of export centers capable of mass production of the low technology items by which Japan first established itself as a leader. Singapore, Taiwan, Hong Kong, Thailand, the Philippines and South Korea are the major centers; Sri Lanka, under its new regime, seems headed in the same direction. These new centers bring together hardworking and inexpensive labor with the massive demand for textiles, ready-to-wear clothing, appliances, small electronic items, and other consumer goods that the markets of the developed nations provide.

Authoritarian governments and enterprise methods co-exist in the regimes of the export centers. Aside from the inherent instability of such methods of governance, these economies are extremely vulnerable to any downward turn in the Western economies, for whom their exports are destined.

The Attack at Home

It is tempting to read the relative quietude of the United States as an indication of a healthy climate for the enterprise system. Terrorist bombings are comparatively rare; the mass protests of the previous decade have vanished; socialist and communist political activity is probably at its lowest level in this century. OPEC's price spiral is causing some significant dislocation within the economy, but various remedies are being pursued. In comparison with other parts of the world, the United States seems safe and secure for private enterprise.

The perceptive observer, however, will not mistake the atypical character of the U.S. political climate as a reassurance against attack. It has been pointed out that the most influential political party in the United States of the last forty years is the Socialist Party: almost every plank of its 1932 platform is now law, and those who studied political science in 1932 will remember that then every plank in the 1912 platform of the Progressive Party had become law.

In view of these remarks, it is interesting to consider whether or not the recent platforms of the Socialist Party U.S.A., and the Socialist Workers Party also presage the changes of the future. Thus what are we to make of the 1976 Socialist Party U.S.A. platform proposal on the economy:

"Inflation, unfair taxes, rising unemployment, the declining quality of consumer goods, and the neglect of our society's real needs are symptoms of capitalism that affect us. Only social control of the production and distribution of goods will create the base for building a new society. Neither

18

reactionary economists nor capitalist advocates of governmental spending pretend any longer even to have temporary solutions to the continuing decline in real wages and job opportunities. Social control of banking and credit has become an immediate pressing need."

Likewise consider the following platform plank on workers' control:

"A goal of the Socialist Party is workers' control of all industry through democratic organization of the work-place, with workers making all the decisions now made by management. The Socialist Party proposes a society of free, continuing, and democratic participation through shop councils, and through councils for the management of each industry by workers and others most affected by it, including consumers. Spheres of life other than industry should also have popular control. These are the bases for democratic socialism, and can be achieved only through radical social change."

"The Socialist party supports moves toward democratic decision making, whether in private or government enterprise, which genuinely limits management authority by institutionalizing power in the hands of working people and their democratic organizations. We favor, in general, an increase in the decision making power of work groups."[3]

Or we might consider some of the proposals of the 1972 Socialist Workers Party platform. They propose to:

"Organize committees of the unions and consumer groups with the power to regulate prices."

"Abolish all taxes on incomes under $10,000 a year. Confiscate all profits on war goods. A 100 per cent tax on incomes above $25,000 per year."

"Roll back all rents on apartments to a maximum of 10 per cent of family income."

"Expropriate the major corporations and banks and operate them under the control of democratically elected workers committees. Plan the economy democratically for the benefit of all instead of for the profit of the few."

"Bring to power a workers government, with full recognition of the right of self-determination to the oppressed to reorganize America on a socialist basis."

They are for:

"Free quality medical and dental care for all, through the socialization of medicine."

"A nationally coordinated program to build safe, efficient, comfortable mass public transit systems. All mass transit to be free."

"A 100 per cent tax on every cent in profits made by the polluters. All corporations to be compelled, under threat of confiscation, to install pollution-control equipment and to meet standards set and enforced by committees of workers and consumers."[4]

Is this to be the wave of the future? It is a chilling question.

Historically, the United States has always been distinctive in its political evolution, standing apart in significant ways from the patterns followed by its European cousins. Because the United States is, historically speaking, a young nation, it has continuities and developmental patterns very different from the European nations where historical institutions have been added, layer upon layer, to very ancient foundations. While this nation may lack some of the exquisite charm of great chateaux and majestic cathedrals, it has also been spared some of the difficulties that come with encrusted social strata, each of which makes claims upon the political order.

Thus, while it may be true that there is a "power structure" or "establishment" at the summit of U.S. society, it is a relatively open, responsive, and evolving elite; to a greater extent than is true in Europe, entry is geared to education, intelligence, and commitment. In Europe, such flexibility is not possible, since the pinnacles of social and financial influence frequently draw on centuries of institutionalized access to important centers of decision making. America's few extremely wealthy families could not, even if they wished to, exercise the kind of control that can be wielded by the great financial, landed, aristocratic, ecclesiastical, or industrial families of Europe. And the contrast is only sharpened when one compares the vast continental marketing and production system of the United States to Europe's tightly concentrated civilization: not only does the United States have few whose inherited position makes a great deal of difference, but this nation's vastness dilutes their potential impact.

The notion that anyone can rise to greatness in America is, of course, part of our national lore, but there are practical political consequences of relative openness or accessibility of entry to the "establishment." For our purposes, the most significant is the relatively low level of ideological content in national political debate. European society, by its highly stratified character, has encouraged the development of ideological stances; children of workers tend to become workers themselves to a greater extent than is true in the United States, and this stable class order encourages political identities along class lines. The absence of proletarian politics in America is not because there is no working class, but because working people have never identified themselves as permanently bound to a fixed status level.

It has been important for the development of the enterprise system in the United States that we have been relatively free of the shackles of ideological infighting. It is thought that energy spent debating which worldview should dominate the government structure is counterproductive and detracts from the capacity of the enterprise system to "get things done"; this view has been at the center of our national and global success.

However, this strength of our political order should not be allowed to mask the incipient problems the enterprise system faces. The low level of the voices calling for the abolition of the system does not mean that there are not forces or trends within the very workings of the current structure that can undermine the enterprise system. No political party of individuals need demand the collapse of enterprise in order for patterns of public and governmental behavior, if left unattended, to undermine the foundations on which that order operates.

A New Class?

Some current discussions of private versus public management of the economy focus on the role of a "New Class" in the growing role of government. Analysts of various political colorations find "new classes" from time to time—Milovan Djilas, a Yugoslav writer, detected a "new class" in Stalinist Russia, and was imprisoned for his views; in the 1960s, New Left theorists in the United States and Europe talked of a "new working class" of technical and service-oriented people. The latest formulation, popularized by Irving Kristol, identifies the New Class as a set of people who regularly and persistently attack the corporate character of our economy from the safety of government and university posts, protected enclaves that ultimately rely on corporate productivity for their survival.

Kristol's argument has some merit—clearly there are loud and persistent voices seeking to arouse the public on a wide range of issues that affect corporate profitability and policy-making. The environmental movement, to cite just one example, has already had a multi-billion dollar impact on U.S. industry through its publicity and lobbying activities.

But should this kind of activity be regarded as the program of a "new class" that seeks to undermine business and increase government regulation? While it is tempting to give the pro-regulation forces a label, and to ascribe to that "New Class" all the current difficulties between business and government, this approach runs serious risks. Earlier in this decade, Peter Drucker argued that the consumer movement had arisen because business had failed to comprehend what the consumer values—to his mind, consumerism is the "shame of marketing."[5] In a similar vein, to the extent that pro-regulation sentiment reflects real and widespread social concerns, attempts to label it and dismiss it as the efforts of ungrateful intellectuals can only cause greater public alienation and further isolate business. Deeper social trends must be analyzed to explain our current crisis.

Legacy of a Decade of Protest

Research of opinion analysts indicates that political and social opinion underwent a profound shift in the 1960s. The focus of the daily newscasts was on the issues that divided public opinion: minority rights and Vietnam. At the same time, a more significant shift was occurring in the fundamental political perceptions of the nation. Detected as a long-term trend by the major polling organizations, there has been a substantial downward shift in public confidence in all the major institutions of our society. A recently released study entitled *The Evaluations of Basic American Institutions with Special Reference to Business*, by Seymour Martin Lipset and William Schneider, cites a poll showing that public confidence in the leadership of nine different institutions was cut nearly in half over the past decade: 41 percent of the population had "a great deal of confidence" in 1966, but that percentage slipped down to the low 20s by 1977.[6]

The institutions for which confidence in leadership was measured constitute an interesting cross-section of U.S. society. They include:

- medicine
- organized religion
- the press
- the military
- the Supreme Court
- the Executive Branch
- Congress
- labor unions
- major companies

Confidence in the leadership of business, it should be noted, fell somewhat more than confidence in the leadership of other institutions. The average decline for the leadership of the above institutions was 19 percentage points, while business fell by 32 points. Starting from an above-average level of confidence in 1966 (55 percent), business has remained below the average level since 1972. Thus, the leadership of the business community is faced with a rather ominous warning concerning its own future credibility with the public.

A more general concern is warranted as well, however, because of the wide range of institutions in the above list. The decline, it is evident, affects both public and private institutions of our society. Other studies indicate that various important private elements of society—educators, lawyers, scientists—have also fallen in public esteem in this period. We are facing, in other words, a system-wide decline in popular confidence in the leadership of the very institutions by which the nongovernmental aspect of society (as well as the governmental) is organized.

To some extent, this shift can be identified as public

alienation from particular leaders. The revelations of the Watergate era tarnished not only the reputation of Richard Nixon, but also that of the Presidency itself. Still, there is a considerable difference between the confidence in an individual and the confidence in an institution, and people understand the difference. A severe windstorm can wreak havoc on a village, a town, or even a region, but it will not alter the patterns of the world's climate on which the survival of humankind depends; similarly, a nation can endure serious fluctuations in confidence in its leaders if the broader structure of social institutions still commands the respect and loyalty of the people.

Our current crisis, however, is at that deeper level of institutional stability. Current trends in public attitudes are producing major structural changes in the relationship between government and the private sector, between public power and private initiative. And the changes, it is quite clear, will come at the expense of individual rights, business prerogatives, and ultimately the well-being of the entire private aspect of our national life.

Public Attitudes toward Government

The current crisis is compounded by another factor: the increased reliance on government regulation. Although, as we have seen, government has also suffered from a decline in public confidence, this loss of respect is not due to a reduction in governmental influence. On the contrary, government has grown throughout this era of declining public prestige.

How has this come about? Much of the growth of government is traceable directly to the protests of the 1960s and early 1970s. In the wake of protests, various measures were enacted that were intended to *redress partic-*

ular grievances of a constitutional nature: equal opportunity, voting rights, and other anti-discriminatory legislation. In one sense, these particular reforms were essentially conservative in that they sought to right the balance between the individual and the state where there have been noticeable inequities, but for the most part, they were fought for and won by liberals. Other measures taken were intended to *remedy political and social problems:* electoral campaign reforms, the National Environmental Protection Act, and OSHA (the Occupational Safety and Health Act).

In both kinds of issues, the result has been the same: increased government control. Although government itself was one of the prime targets for the discontent of the 1960s, it has also turned out to be the prime instrumentality by which solutions to problems in nongovernmental areas have been sought. Thus, we are faced with a paradoxical situation in which the net result of an outburst of anti-public-sector sentiment has been a further strengthening of that sector's overall power.

The Pattern of Dependency

It is likely that most Americans would recoil in horror at the prospect of an all-powerful government that was free to dictate how each citizen lived his daily life, that monitored and regulated his every movement, and that prescribed in minute detail the limits within which he could seek to maximize his own well-being. The spectre of "big brother government" is still a disturbing image in our national political mind.

And yet, the public seems willing to abide steady incremental increases in the power of government. The Lipset-Schneider study cited previously indicates that a consistent majority of the public, while aware of the ever-increasing extent of government controls, is opposed to any reduction. It appears that whatever distrust the public has of government, it is not as high as that felt toward the business community.

To some extent, this frame of mind may be an inevitable element of the American mentality. As has been remarked, "The problem with Americans is that they haven't read the minutes of the last meeting." To paraphrase Schumpeter, the secular improvement in everyday life over the last 200 years is profound—but no one lives for 200 years. We are all short-term phenomena, and the immediate afflictions of job insecurity or inflation weigh more heavily than our recollections of the not-so-distant past. Life may be better for the clerk or factory operative than it was for his father, but he is more likely to contrast his modest income with the great fortunes accumulated by the relatively few. Schumpeter sums it up well: "Secular improvement that is taken for granted and coupled with individual insecurity that is acutely resented is of course the best recipe for breeding social unrest."[7] And widespread social unrest, of course, may be viewed as the best recipe for turning to government to cure all ills.

Restraints on Business

In the struggle for popular allegiance, there are some severe limitations on the way in which the business community can participate. Much is made of the political power of "big business," yet politicians, largely out of fear of how the media will portray them, will avoid support for business-initiated proposals, no matter how sound such proposals may be from a public interest standpoint. A desire to avoid mixing a firm's economic well-being with political controversy also contributes to the relatively low profile business maintains in the public eye. The power of "big business" in political terms is, comparatively speaking, not very "big."

Business leaders also tend to avoid competition in public arenas with important elements of the opinion-making community—journalists, professors, clergymen, philosophers, and other intellectually-oriented professionals. This reluctance is understandable, given the pressure of pragmatic business affairs, yet it means that the role of business interests in the formation of public consciousness on issues of the day is diminished.

Several decades ago, Berle and Means alerted us to the transition then under way in which the control of firms was shifting from owners to managers. Now there is a new transition: control by managers is giving way to control by government regulation. In effect, government has begun to operate as an "invisible management" within the business community—and with increasingly disastrous results.

The Political Payments Law

The workings of this "invisible government" permeate the business dealings of every large and small corporation in the United States. The following is but one example.

Recently, a piece of legislation extended the invisible hand of government to the overseas dealings of U.S. firms through the political payments law. The already-appearing consequences of this law are great, and provide a good example of how treacherous the present political environment can be for the business corporations of this country.

The political payments law was quite clearly an "after-shock" of the Watergate earthquake, and the media paid considerable attention to the general issue of payments to officials in high places by U.S. corporations. Embarrassing revelations about high government officials abroad set off tremors felt throughout the nation's major institutions and those abroad as well. These revelations about payments to foreign leaders in contract negotiations led to the passage of legislation that required new auditing procedures within U.S. corporations and new legal definitions of acceptable forms of payments abroad.

What the law gained in political righteousness (an important consideration for our political leaders, whose reputations were tarnished by Watergate), it sacrificed in economic practicality. Through this law, the U.S. government regulates some new aspects of U.S. corporations' relations with foreign countries and businesses. These regulations are an expression of the ethical standards that the American public presumably wants imposed on business conducted by U.S. companies operating abroad.

But it is well known that foreign business relations regularly involve a wide range of facilitative payments, and that businesses have treated these payments as an "entry cost" to be factored into any investment decision. The government's decision to legislate the application of American morality to all U.S. business abroad can only reduce the ability of U.S. firms to compete in the world arena, without affecting whatsoever the moral standards of international business negotiations. The net results of this particular "reform" measure are to enhance the regulatory burden carried by U.S. firms, expand the number of government regulators on the public payroll, and diminish the effectiveness of U.S. firms in world markets.

Outcomes of this kind are all too typical of the impact of present tendencies of government action. For the business community, already saddled with a variety of serious problems, an added level of government encroachment is both unwelcome and meddlesome. Unless a new relationship can be established between government and business, and new resourcefulness tapped by the private sector of the society generally, the current pessimistic outlook for the private enterprise system will only grow darker.

Measures to reverse this restriction are under way as this essay goes to press. A White House task force has estimated that the United States is losing $1 billion a year in trade because of these restrictions and has recommended eventual abandonment of the restrictions.[8]

Conclusion

The foregoing analysis of the global pressures, forces, and trends threatening the future of the enterprise system is certainly not an optimistic one.

The strengths of our method and form of economic organization are evident in the historical record. Those nations whose economic evolution first brought about the legal structures, social values, and business institutions by which private enterprise developed have enjoyed unparalleled economic success and vast global influence in the past. Yet in the most venerable centers of enterprise, the calls for an alternative economic order—one dominated by the state—are strong enough to make the future of private initiative questionable.

And in those regions of the world where the enterprise system is not indigenous, we find—with the exception of Japan—either unsettled cultures with a marked hostility to the market economies, or pro-enterprise states with authoritarian rulers. Neither of these alternatives gives cause for hope.

The United States, where the enterprise system has come of age and where its global extension has reached new heights, is faced with a continual erosion of public confidence—a collective nervous breakdown, so to speak —in all aspects of its political, social, and economic behavior. While the business community has been a prime victim of this declining esteem, the pervasiveness of the decline is an indication of a general crisis for the private sector of society.

Accompanying this decline has been a significant increase in the reach and sheer mass of governmental power. Government regulation has been the goal of the reformers, who have dominated the political headlines since the late 1950s, when political protest and social unrest began to remake the nation's political consciousness.

Thus, the absence of a highly visible socialist/communist movement here is simply the absence of a *familiar* symbol of enterprise under attack, rather than an indication that there is no attack at all—indeed, the attack is quite robust, if widely dispersed.

It is obvious that in this brief account of the state of the world enterprise system, we must be extremely selective in what we consider. The purpose of this account has been to provide a realistic basis for prescribing changes in the way in which our society—and the business community in particular—responds to the present malaise. There is no pleasure associated with a recitation of complex problems or unpleasant prospects: one plumbs the depths of such issues in order to prepare the way for meaningful response.

The challenge to the enterprise system will be met successfully only if its leadership is willing to recognize that such issues can only be resolved in our modern world on a global scale. The well-being of each nation's people is still the prime responsibility of its own leaders; the fate of each people is so intertwined, however, that only those individuals farsighted enough to accept the responsibilities of global interdependence will actually succeed in this basic mission.

For the enterprise system, this global context demands that business leadership show the same adaptive genius demonstrated in other eras in the history of our society. New understanding will require new forms of organization, new approaches to other cultures, and a new (and more balanced) relationship of businesses and national governments, both here and abroad.

Notes

1.   Orin Atkins, Chairman of the Board and Chief Executive Officer, Ashland Oil, Inc., noted in a September 19, 1979, talk to the American Society for Industrial Security, held in Detroit, that we have now had our "first recorded hijacking of an oil tanker. This incident occurred in July in Thailand. A group of armed men stowed away on the ship, overpowered the crew and siphoned off some 2,000 gallons of diesel fuel to a waiting fishing trawler. The tanker had been carrying 120,000 gallons of diesel.

"As the prices of both crude oil and petroleum products continue to rise, more hijacking incidents can be expected. With criminals, especially terrorists, apparently undaunted even by heavy security measures, it is very likely that there will be more attempts on tankers or other isolated oil transportation facilities. The temptation is great—and crude oil bears no identifying marks."

2.   Henry A. Kissinger, "Communist Parties in Western Europe: Challenge to the West," in *Eurocommunism: The Italian Case*, edited by Austin Raney and Giovanni Sartori (Washington, D.C.: American Enterprise Institute for Policy Research, 1978), p. 186.

3.   "Socialist Party U.S.A. 1976 Platform," pamphlet.

4.   "Socialist Workers Platform 1972," in Donald B. John-

son and Kirk H. Porter, *National Party Platforms*, 5th ed. (University of Illinois, 1972), pp. 885–889.

5.   Peter F. Drucker, *Management: Tasks, Responsibilities, Practices* (New York: Harper and Row, 1976), p. 64.

6.   Seymour Martin Lipset and William Schneider, *The Evaluation of Basic American Institutions with Special Reference to Business*, 1979, pp. 15–21, *passim.*

7.   Joseph A. Schumpeter, *Capitalism, Socialism and Democracy*, Part II.

8.   *New York Times*, June 12, 1979.

2

Philosophical Dimensions

THE development of an adequate strategy for the survival and strengthening of the enterprise system must
consider the elements of its past success, but it cannot
rely solely on them. Too often proponents of our economic
order have believed that simply identifying and returning
to the philosophical concepts and the values that served
well in the past—free markets, competition, government
restraint, voluntary actions, hard work, perseverance,
diligence, respect for law—could reinvigorate the entire
system. While a clear understanding of the philosophical
dimensions on which the enterprise system is based will
not itself guarantee its survival, it is a necessary precon-
dition to designing the proper strategies for the future.

And the private enterprise system cannot be understood apart from its historical roots in Western society. As
we have seen in the previous section, the non-Western
world has created some adaptations of enterprise methods, but with fairly limited success because of the absence of many of the social and political factors that have

been supportive of the enterprise system in the West. Hybrid systems have been produced in which the economic methodology of the West has been grafted onto a social order that remains virtually unchanged.

However, the *political* and *social* values that have accompanied the rise of the enterprise economies of the West are highly *respected*—if not practiced—throughout the world. Individual rights, constitutionalism, and democratic government are the watchwords of peoples all over the world—including the socialist countries of Eastern Europe. Even the leaders of the Vietnamese revolution borrowed a page from the American Declaration of Independence in drafting the constitution of their new nation.

In this section, the sources of the vitality of the enterprise system will be explored. The continued success of the Western societies and the potential for successful outreach onto the global stage by their system depend on the creative utilization of the energy, drive, and motivation that our political order is able to unleash. A two-fold application of these principles of social and economic organization will be considered:

- *the social nexus:* how private rights affect the political order
- *the corporate nexus:* how "private governments" can draw upon the principles of the public order

The Changing Character of Private Property

The idea of private property is basic to our culture. In its Latin root, *proprius,* property is directly tied to the person, the individual. Just as a "proper noun" refers to a person, so "proper-ty" is linked to individuality, to a person's "own-ness." Our use of the phrase "private property" is, in historical perspective, a redundancy—property is inherently private. (When we speak of "public property," we are referring to that which is owned by a "public person"—the state.) John Locke, the English philosopher who helped shape our political order, understood this fundamental notion of property when he stated: "By *Property* I must be understood here, as in other places, to mean that Property which Men have in their Persons as well as Goods."[1]

In our present situation, some slippage has occurred in this relationship between property and the person. Two forces are changing the conceptual landscape: the power of the state and the evolution of economic institutions.

The governmental impact on property rights is evident to everyone. Zoning laws placed limitations on the use of property as urban areas grew in the early years of this century; more recently, environmental restrictions have added another series of constraints. Rental property is subject to many restrictions in municipalities across the country, ranging from permissible rents to tenant rights —as a most recent trend, there are restrictions as well on the right to sell rental units as condominiums.

In economic or financial matters, the relationship between ownership and the exercise of the rights of ownership has become increasingly vague. The expansion of ownership, which has come with the growth in the number of stockholders nationally—and internationally—has facilitated the rise of managers who are not significant owners. Pension trust funds, mutual funds, and other complex financial structures have added to the perplexing layering of claims by which modern business organizations operate. The traditional image of a small entrepreneur who owned his business, met his payroll, and reaped the profits of his efforts is descriptive now mainly of relatively small companies.

However, private enterprise *is* a manifestation of *pri-*

vate property. The capital that establishes and supports a business is owned by the stockholders (who are individuals and institutions) and not by the state. Decisions about running the business are made by the board of directors and the officers, not by government functionaries and bureaucracies. The search for profit drives the company; the search for increased income drives the officers; and this results in competition among the companies in an industry to claim as much of the market as possible.

The future of private enterprise is clearly part of the more general question of the future of private property itself. It would appear that, in the Western world, a slow erosion of the traditional concept of private property is under way. The notion that an individual could possess something utterly beyond the power of the state, that ownership was (almost) inherent and inalienable, is one that has lost some considerable degree of assent today. Perhaps it will turn out that in a world of material abundance, absolute ownership will no longer seem as important as it did in a world characterized by scarcity.

Whatever the social and psychological causes, the sense of private property—indeed, the sense of privacy in general—seems to be weakening. From an economic perspective, this weakening is manifested in the development of a number of forms of property beyond the immediate control of the individual: many investment and savings accounts, pension funds, social security, and medical health programs. Other factors that weaken private property are the high taxes on the highest income brackets and the tendency toward more and more confiscatory estate taxes. The right to inherit has been a traditional support of private property, but more and more frequently it is the state that inherits the estate.

This evolution in the concept of private property has major implications for modern business. Government regulation has clearly played a part in bringing about this evolution, but it also is evident that modern business practices, responding to the pressures of an evolving technology, and public demands, have also contributed to the change. The task for the present is to sort out the implications of this change for the relation of the individual to the government and discover how, by extension, this affects the relationship of modern business to the public sector.

The Private Sector

Government, in the "liberal" Western philosophic tradition, is seen as an agreement by which the freedom of individuals is maximized through the common acceptance of limitations on all. The governmental entity—the public sector—exists only to augment or enhance nongovernmental activity—the private sector.

Understood in this sense, the private sector includes all those aspects of social life that have not been ceded or delegated by the citizens to the government. An enormous range of meaningful human activities thus falls under the general rubric of the private sector. They include:

- the multi-faceted life of the family
- the internal life of the local community
- the welfare activities of indigenous groups within the community
- the various private educational bodies (private schools, colleges, and universities)
- the healers of body and soul
- the religious institutions of all faiths
- the associations of professionals of all kinds (scholars, artists, writers, lawyers)
- the labor unions
- the business enterprises

In essence, any voluntary association through which human beings seek to fulfill their goals—spiritual or material, altruistic or self-directed—constitutes an activity of the private sector.

In its completely voluntary character, the private sector is distinguished from the public sector. In most things governmental, the rule of law applies, and usually a coercive element is implicit in its workings. In Western societies, the best yardstick for measuring the relative freedom of the people is to see how strongly the right of free association is respected, for it is on that right that the private sector rests. If individuals are free to take initiatives to further their own well-being and that of others with whom they choose to join, the society will enjoy the benefits of their activity, and the private sector will thrive. To the extent that government interposes restrictions on the kinds and activities of associations—religious, economic, political, even familial—that are permissible, it limits the free flow of human creativity.

Rights of property are clearly linked to the private sector. In the fundamental meaning of property discussed earlier, a person's capabilities are an important possession, and the exercise of personal talents is synonymous with the exercise of property rights. States may attempt to deprive citizens of these basic properties—through censorship, restrictions on economic activity, and so on—but frequently other routes are found: black markets, underground presses, and smuggling commonly escalate in societies where barriers have been erected to the free activity of the nation's citizens.

The concern over the nature of government encroachment on the private sector, which was examined in the earlier section, is not simply a question of economic policy. A fundamental relationship between the individual and his society is at stake in the balance between private and public sectors, and one that cannot be seriously altered without the gravest of implications for the structure of political and personal freedom under which we live.

The Prophets of Doom

Some schools of thought claim that this loss of freedom is inherent in the workings of our economic system. At various points in the evolution of capitalism, analysts have argued that there will inevitably come a point at which the private enterprise system will so thoroughly undermine its own foundations that it will bring about its own demise.

Marx is the most famous of capitalism's critics, and an early prophet of its ultimate collapse. Marx claimed that his case against capitalism was not a matter of personal animosity for this economic order (though he made no effort to disguise his dislike of it) but of iron-clad laws of historical change. For Marxist revolutionaries throughout the world, this faith that the future is theirs—that the fate of capitalism is already determined—has been an important strategic weapon.

Marx's description of the rise of capitalism showed important factors in the relationships between social change and economic behavior. His writings on the transition from feudal to capitalist society were a significant achievement. But, Marx's inadequacy was to try to extend his analysis of the historical patterns of the past into the future. His anticipation of the collapse of capitalism has not turned out as he expected: not a single advanced capitalist nation has yet passed through the stages of decline and revolutionary upheaval that he predicted. Russia, the first country to undergo a revolution in which Marxist leadership took power, was at that time the *least* developed of all the major European nations; Lenin and Trotsky went to great pains to justify the seizure of power by the self-proclaimed vanguard of the working class in a country that was over 85 percent peasants.

Marxism has been an influential force in Western Europe, as we saw earlier, but only in the developing world has it served as a revolutionary credo. The theoretical acrobatics necessary to explain how Asian peasants, nomadic desert tribesmen, and Latin American guerrillas can fulfill the communist destiny are perhaps not to be taken seriously, but Marx's predictions for an advanced capitalist society are still taken seriously by many, and define a goal that attracts many of the dissatisfied.

Joseph Schumpeter was a different kind of political philosopher—his views were essentially conservative, and he was strongly sympathetic toward capitalism. And yet he too expressed serious doubts about the ability of our economic order to survive its own internal dynamics. Writing in 1942, he doubted the system's ability to survive more than one or two generations.

Schumpeter cited two difficulties that he believed might be fatal: both are of interest to us in the present context.

First, Schumpeter pointed to the size of large corporations. As the size of private business organizations grew, they would come to resemble in many ways the deadly bureaucracies of the large governmental structures. Personal initiative would lose in importance to hierarchical politics; distances from real decision-making centers would increase, diminishing the incentive for individuals to try to make their own views known. Gradually, big business grows to mirror, in every respect, the public sector, until it makes little difference to employees whether they serve in one or the other. At that point, popular allegiance to the enterprise system is so neutralized that the innate tendency of public bureaucracy to expand is irreversible.

Schumpeter's second concern was intimately related to the first. As corporations increase in size, he argued, they tend not only to replicate the public bureaucracies, but tend also to take over the activities of smaller firms:

> . . . the perfectly bureaucratized giant industrial unit not only ousts the small or medium-sized firm and "expropriates" its owners, but in the end it also ousts the entrepreneur and "expropriates" the bourgeoisie as a class which in the process stands to lose not only its income, but also what is infinitely more important, its function.[2]

Thus, Schumpeter argues, the large firm will not only reduce its employees to so many cogs in a machine, but the machine will gobble up all those outside who would carry on the entrepreneurial spirit. All in all, a rather dismal prospect for the societies with capitalist roots.

Philosophical discussions can be useful if they stimulate thought and provoke new insights. Schumpeter clearly foresaw trends in our society that could reduce a culture built on individual initiative to a tiresome, boring, and monolithic order, and it is valuable to consider his argument in thinking of strategies for the future. The problems cited should be seen as components of a challenge that needs to be met by the leadership of the current generation. Both of Schumpeter's points relate to the governance of the large corporation, and it is to those issues that this philosophical component of the discussion now turns.

Constitutionalism

From the earlier discussion of the private sector, it is evident that the maintenance of freedom in a society depends on the strength and vigor of the nongovernmental elements in the society. The necessity for government is incontrovertible, but government must be balanced by strong capacities for private initiative if the society is to avoid authoritarian extremes.

This system of balances between governmental sectors is an essential component of constitutional systems of government. In the U.S. Constitution, it is evident that the Founding Fathers went to great lengths to set up "checks and balances" so that the aberrations of any particular element of government could be corrected by the actions of the others. Underlying that principle was the notion that no one group of people, nor any one interest, can provide perfect justice for an entire society. Constitutional government limits the power of those governing by providing counterbalances to any particular power that it grants. By structuring governmental prerogatives in such a way that each element holds some sway over the others, a constitutional regime ensures that there is no top roost, no pinnacle from which any given voice can rule by absolute fiat.

There are times, it should be acknowledged, when even a constitutional system grants special powers to its rulers. A state of war is a classic example: faced with military conflict, a legislative body can grant "war powers" to the executive in the interest of ensuring the most highly coordinated and unified response to the external threat. Such power is always limited in duration, however, out of natural suspicion that it might otherwise become the basis for a permanent increase in the powers of one branch of government.

The underlying rationale for this rather complex balancing act we call constitutional rule is that it maximizes the extent to which the people of the society—the governed—can participate in the process of governing. The limitations on the powers of each element of government at even the highest level mean that the interests and well-being of the governed supersede any particular interest of the state. By denying, through structural constraints, the pinnacle of power to any one individual, party, or interest, the constitutional system implicitly installs the common interest—what Rousseau, the philosopher-king of the French Revolution, called the "general will"—on the throne of power.

Corporations as Fictional Persons

Some of the "people" who participate in the development of the social consensus or "general will" are not people in anything but a legal sense. These are the corporations, the "fictional persons" that have existed within the Western community since early times. A corporation is an entity without a body, a legal fiction created by individuals who choose to associate with each other for some purpose of common interest. We treat it as a person and assign to it many of the legal claims and obligations of a real person.

Our society is full of corporations. Though in common parlance the term "corporation" is frequently used to refer to a business, almost every institution of our society is incorporated. Universities are corporations; religious institutions are, as well; scientific, cultural, and political organizations also incorporate in order to establish their legal presence. In fact, the corporation is deeply enmeshed in our social fabric, in the exercise of property rights, in the national decision-making process, and in the distribution of authority among social institutions. The corporation can only exist within the context of a legal system, which in turn implies the existence of a state. The state, though in this sense legally prior to the corporation, in general permits corporations to live out their lives on their own initiative, subject only to the restrictions of law.

The crucial characteristic of corporations in functional terms is the voluntary character of the association. Like the constitutional system described earlier, the corporation in modern society is an expression of a decision to join in a relationship with defined limitations for mutual benefit.

Private Governments

Within the various corporations (as well as in the broader set of associational voluntary relationships), principles of governance are at work. The principles, of course, will vary from setting to setting, but there are always certain common elements, whether in the Boy Scouts or a major multinational corporation. Some of these elements are:

- a set of rules and regulations
- plans or programs
- expectancies
- a common framework for discourse
- some common understanding of the collective purpose

Furthermore, there is always some interplay between the formal decision-making structures of an association and the informal ones; friendships, alliances, caucuses, parties, and liaisons of every conceivable sort impinge upon the methods of every organization, making every group activity political in some sense.

The private sector, then, cannot rightly be thought of as so many atomized individuals, but as a mass of associational ties that create a vast overlapping and intertwined network or collectivity. Like public government, this system of private governments is a means of distributing power and authority within the society. The constant evolution of society means that power is always shifting; new associations spring up, energized by the interest or dedication of their members. Various elements compete for standing within this private arena. No formal constitutional structure exists within which this change occurs, other than the limitations set by the legal statutes of the nation. Essentially, however, the private governments carry out many of the same kinds of responsibilities that we see performed by the public sector in a constitutional regime.

Revising the Equation

The many forces discussed in the first part have altered the historical content of these concepts in ways that suggest some fundamental revision is now in order. Briefly stated, a new equation must be found by which the principles and methods of governance operable in both private and public settings can be applied for the protection and furtherance of personal freedom in its social, political, and economic dimensions.

A key element in this new equation will be the elaboration of a theory of private corporate government, since it is within the large modern business corporation that the great responsibilities of our economic welfare and the challenge of the defense of a system of political values come together.

The development of a satisfactory theory of private corporate government will probably require the cooperative efforts of both the academy and the corporation. They must both be involved in the theoretical analysis and in the practical observations of corporate governance in action. But there are obstacles. Political scientists, with rare exceptions, have been so fascinated with the majesty of the state that they take little notice of other polities. Economists, with perhaps more frequent exceptions, become preoccupied with the nonpolitical aspects of corporate enterprise.

Facing Governmental Reality

The necessary functions of public government for advanced societies constitute one element that has shifted in our basic equation. It is now widely accepted among leaders of major business corporations that some governmental involvement is a permanent aspect of the economic environment. It is argued that certain technological features of our advanced age create such problems for the basic security and stability of the society that government must be present in an oversight capacity. The problems stemming from plutonium and other radioactive materials are among the most pressing cases raised; easy access to material that could be used to blackmail an entire civilization is too fundamental a security issue to dismiss lightly as a matter of governmental meddling. Similarly, disease and pest control, an important element of life in a world where intercontinental travel is frequent and food production highly concentrated, is hard to envision without coordination by governmental bodies.

The essential question, of course, is the extent to which matters of somewhat less than a life-and-death nature justify an expanded role for government. Advocates of government will insist that every element of social activity is, in some sense, vital and, therefore, a required realm of regulation. While resisting pressures for *general* government expansion, the business community and its allies throughout the private sector must confront in a realistic manner—as has occurred at the executive levels of some of the largest industrial sectors—the question of a governmental presence in *specific* areas that are crucial to maintaining a stable global society.

Public sentiment at present holds that large-scale government is necessary in a number of problem areas, and business can enhance its own reputation by recognizing the perceived seriousness of the problems. The recognition that government involvement is inevitable in a number of important policy issues will also improve business' ability to challenge encroachment in areas outside that restricted realm.

A Corporate Theory of World Order

The question of a revised definition of the role of public government in our era should not be treated apart from its broader relation to political theory. It is possible that a new conception of the role of government will be one part of a theory of business governance that will constitute a new and important chapter in the history of political theory itself. It should not be forgotten that political science was enriched in the late Middle Ages and the early modern period by profound studies of the governance of the church—the dominant social institution of the time. And, the bases of ecclesiastical governance greatly influenced the theory of modern constitutionalism.

Corporate governance may well assume something of the same significance for the latter part of the twentieth century and the beginning of the twenty-first century that ecclesiastical governance had for reconciling the problems of church and state in the sixteenth and seventeenth centuries. The highest levels of corporate leadership have in their hands today the raw materials for another great period of insight and breakthrough, one of truly global dimensions. As the great church councils of the past introduced patterns of theory and practice that profoundly influenced the development of Western parliamentary institutions, so may the business corporation of the future bring forth theory and practice that will shape many social patterns of the future. Great corporate leadership could influence the pattern of law and order in the marketplace of the community of nations. Such leadership could influence the basic ways of adjusting conflicting interests within nations. And finally, such leadership could help to crystallize more meaningful and operational concepts of human freedom.

Governance of the Large Corporation

All great institutions of civilizations past and present have applied some form of internal governance. Whatever the institutional purpose and design, those which survived the test of time invariably have operated under some internal structure of power. From the United Auto Workers to Harvard University mechanisms for completing the basic tasks of governance have always been used. Each, in addition, has reflected some set of goals.

A corporation's system of private government—its theory and means for distributing power and authority within its realm of influence—meets the following fundamental criteria. At a basic level, its charter and bylaws provide the foundation for the governance structure. The firm's leadership, through its policy decisions, provides another element in the picture; while a body of precedent linked to policy grows and evolves as the firm endures, another aspect of the corporate governmental structure is added. Finally, an unwritten constitution is always present in the form of company customs that are intrinsic to a particular firm—this body of practices is the corporate equivalent of the tradition of the common law in English judicial history.

In addition, a corporation's system of private government must have a fundamental set of objectives: creating a framework of justice within the corporate system, providing a code of business ethics for dealing with the ethical codes of all cultures with which the company has relationships, and, finally, evolving the firm's own theory of social, as well as economic, purposes.

Corporate Constitutionalism

Constitutionalism, as discussed earlier, suggests a set of principles that can be useful in the further elaboration of the internal governance framework of the corporation and in the fulfillment of its fundamental objectives. As we have noted earlier, the constitutional setting should protect the individual from arbitrary acts of government. The mechanism for doing this is the rule of law, the notion that all individuals are equal before the law and deserve equal treatment. In the context of our political order, the emphasis falls most strongly on the presence of law; in corporate settings, the same notion is useful in introducing the concept of set rules. Clearly, business corporations will never attempt to replicate the law-making aspects of public constitutional regimes, but they can establish procedures for rule making.

Such a "quasi-constitutional" approach to making rules can be a significant aid in the firm's relationship with the many outside constituencies with whom its leadership must contend. Though the modern corporation must remain fixed on its economic goals if it is to maintain profitability and growth (and thus insure its survival), it is more and more evident that these outside forces seriously affect the long-term and even short-range profitability of many firms.

The multi-faceted demand structure of the environment within which the modern corporation operates renders inoperable traditional management models that focused on the firm's economic activity as the sole guidepost. Rather, we see in our current political order the objective basis for a pluralistic framework for analyzing corporate decision making. Unless the firm is willing to recognize the need for a systematic method for factoring into the economic policy process the evaluation of this wide range of outside forces—from government regulation to consumer groups, environmental protestors to activist stockholder groups demanding a greater say—the planning procedures will constantly be disrupted by the unexpected incursions of these issues.

It is worthy of note that Derek C. Bok, President of Harvard, recently decided that these new circumstances necessitated a major revision of the curriculum of the Harvard Business School in order to prepare students better for the challenges they face. After citing the same range of challenges and forces discussed here, President Bok reached the following conclusion:

> Under these circumstances, management arguably exists not simply to serve shareholders but to exercise leadership in reconciling the needs of stockholders, customers, employees, and suppliers, along with members of the public and their representatives in government.[3]

The redesigned curriculum of the Harvard Business School will seek to incorporate all those fields of knowledge and inquiry that impinge upon the decision-making process for an executive in the modern corporation. It should be noted that a number of other leading business schools have adopted this position in evolving their curriculums.

The establishment of a corporate constitutional order under which decisions are made and policy guidelines developed can provide a firm with an enhanced input from the many elements that constitute its internal order and with a better understanding of the threats and opportunities it faces from the outside. The regular lines of division of powers and delegation of responsibility and authority that a constitutional regime provides are key to a flexible and responsive decision-making system at the top level of the modern firm. It is toward that set of internal structures that many forward-looking firms are now moving; only time will tell if their adaptation to new circumstances has been timely and sufficient.

The Business-Government Interface

An optimistic scenario would suggest that increased attention to internal corporate governance by corporate leaders would produce some measurable improvement in the plight of the private sector generally. Such changes, however, will realize their true potential only if they are accompanied by a change in the relationship between private corporations and public government.

At present, it seems that public confidence is at about the same—relatively low—level for both business and government. An adversarial mode of interaction between government and business is widely supported because it offers the best protection, it is felt, for the average citizen. All things being equal, this argument has sound constitutional and pluralistic underpinnings, and the notion that business and government should have an arm's length relationship deserves support from the business community, since it is an important factor in maintaining a healthy and independent climate for enterprise.

It is highly questionable, however, whether the present level of acrimony is either necessary or advisable. When public confidence is low, as it is at this time, the public trust in this adversarial relationship is an indication of a generally pessimistic outlook for the society's prospects and for each individual's, as well. *In such circumstances, it is the private sector that suffers more.* As suggested earlier, erosion of confidence in personal initiative only feeds the dependence on government. In an atmosphere of general public distrust of its leaders, increased government encroachment on private initiatives comes about slowly, incrementally, with glacier-like pressure and persistence. Without any suggestion of authoritarian zeal, the public sector can make irreversible inroads on the nation's well-being.

Alexis de Tocqueville, the French philosopher, after visiting the American republic soon after the War of Independence, foresaw this potential form of governmental servitude and described it eloquently:

> . . . after having thus successfully taken each member of the community in its powerful grasp, and fashioned him at will, the supreme power then extends its arm over the whole community. It covers the surface of society with a network of small complicated rules, minute and uniform, through which the most original minds and the most energetic spirits cannot penetrate to rise above the crowd. The will of man is not shattered but softened, bent and guided; men are seldom forced by it to act, but they are constantly restrained from acting. Such a power does not destroy, but it prevents existence; it does not tyrannize, but it compresses, enervates, extinguishes, and stupefies a people, till each nation is reduced to be nothing better than a flock of timid and industrial animals, of which government is the shepherd—I have always thought that servitude of the regular, quiet, and gentle kind which I have just described might be combined

more easily than is commonly believed with some of the outward forms of freedom and that it might even establish itself under the wing of the sovereignty of the people.[4]

Avoiding this dreadful prospect is, needless to say, a major priority for all elements of the private sector. Ways must be found to maintain the fundamental distance and balance our constitutional system mandates while at the same time reducing the energy that goes into needless adversarial posturing by these two great protagonists.

A New Start

The starting point for an improved relationship is an acceptance of the possibility of learning from one another. Irving S. Shapiro, Chairman and Chief Executive Officer of E. I. du Pont de Nemours and Company, summarized the case well at a May 1979 symposium at Harvard University:

> What the nation needs from business and government is an understanding that neither one of those institutions has a monopoly on intelligence or probity, or the wisdom to prescribe all by itself for the public welfare.[5]

Real progress on revising the relationship will require the implementation of an educative strategy in which each element in this conflict could gain insight into the workings of the other. For businessmen, this will mean a greatly increased involvement in the practical aspects of the governmental process. Traditionally, good governmental relations involved a firm establishing personal ties with a few senators or contributing to political campaigns. The new direction being taken by the most advanced firms involves close and careful attention to all the levels of governmental actions that can limit or influence corporate decision making. Committee action, agency reports, research projections and departmental personnel shifts can all have an impact on the legislative process in ways that will be unclear to corporate officers unless they have directed their own organization to attend closely to such issues. State Department diplomatic appointments can greatly affect overseas operations of a firm, and the corporate executive who has detailed and accurate knowledge of the challenges of the post and the skills of the appointee (or, one step earlier, of potential nominees) will be in an advantageous position. These and related questions are discussed in greater detail in the section on "Business Intelligence" in the third part.

A recent study by the Conference Board (1979) indicates that this strategy is receiving serious attention from corporate leadership. Of 400 large corporations polled in a survey, 92 percent indicated that they had increased their political involvement in the last three years.[6] However, the surface has just been scratched; total corporate disbursements through Political Affairs Committees (PAC's) and industry organizations, according to Federal Election Commission figures, were only $40 million by 1978. Considered in relation to the cost of unnecessary (and avoidable) regulation and inefficiencies occasioned by government-business friction, this is simply an insignificant sum.

Government Regulatory Boards

Liberal critics of business often castigate it for the frequency with which its former executives appear on the boards of regulatory agencies and vice versa. As unjustly as businessmen may feel they are treated by government regulators, it is nevertheless true that a significant number of regulators, at some point, wear the hats of the private sector as well.

The flow or exchange of personnel has, in fact, contributed to the stability of our political order. By providing a steady movement of information, orientation, and basic organizational common sense back and forth, the regulatory agencies have been able to fulfill a role as one element in this sorely needed educative process. Without this exchange of personnel, the epochs of great regulatory thrust in our nation's history—the antitrust era, the New Deal, as well as our current surge—might, it can be argued, have caused severe economic disruption. In an atmosphere of great hostility and uncertainty, it is most likely that political instability would also have been heightened.

However, the virtue of this relationship is not evident to all. Current government regulations stipulate that public employees must wait a certain amount of time before joining companies in the private sector with which an employee had certain relationships, thus altering, if not stemming, the flow of talent and knowledge. To achieve the maximum benefits attainable from the regulatory structure for all aspects of the private sector, the business voice must be sharpened and heightened on policy matters relating to the purpose and staffing of these agencies. Through a well-developed strategy for the business community, regulatory relations could enhance not only the standing of particular industries or interests, but that of all the private sector as well.

Interestingly, the public is already convinced that the regulatory process is good for business. According to the Lipset-Schneider study cited earlier, 46 percent of the American public think that regulation protects the interests of business, while 24 percent disagree.[7] If that predisposition could be made an accurate reflection of reality through thoughtful corporate action, the general public also might benefit greatly.

Conclusion

In this section, some fundamental issues facing the enterprise system have been reviewed with the hope that future strategy discussions might start from a realistic assessment of the gravity of the *conceptual* problems (as well as the pragmatic pressures) facing the enterprise system.

Private property can no longer be evoked as the standard for all political battles of the private sector when the concept has undergone such violent mutation over the past forty years. A new rationale, rooted more stably in the constitutional precepts that underlie both our public and private governments, must emerge if the fierce, competitive, and ultimately unproductive clash between business and government is to be overcome.

This emergent concept will only come to fruition if corporate leadership undertakes the difficult task of clarifying its own internal structures of governance and promotes the development of a structure that adequately satisfies the multifaceted challenges of the external environment. The future of private corporate government in the United States will involve a framework of internal corporate justice, and an international code of ethics. From these efforts and these constructs, a social and economic theory of modern corporate enterprise can evolve. Such innovations will not detract from the profit-related activities of the firm but will greatly enhance it; one can point to the extent to which such measures are already being undertaken by a few large, forward-looking corporations.

The much-needed recasting of the government-business relationship will only come about when the level of understanding is enriched by a heightened exposure to each other's perspective through exchanges on informational, personal, and professional levels.

One of our nation's most distinguished theoreticians of economic change, Melvin Moses Knight, foresaw (in 1940) many of the fundamental pressures that would redefine the enterprise system of the West in our era. In his *Introduction to Economic History*, he summed up the transition:

> An Occidental form of society steeped in the habit and philosophy of acceleration must now learn to decelerate—to "drive in traffic," so to speak.[8]

It remains to be seen whether this deceleration will be a calamitous moment for the West or—preferably—a period of transmutation by which some basic values and beliefs that continue to galvanize the spirits of people throughout the world will provide a basis for adaptation and new growth. Part of "driving in traffic" involves a much closer look at the activities of the surrounding drivers: in the section that follows, some strategies are presented by which the attentiveness of the large business corporation can be enhanced, and its contribution to the health of private behavior in general expanded.

Notes

1. John Locke, *Two Treatises on Government*, Second Treatise, section 173. For a more detailed discussion of this topic, see C. B. MacPherson, *The Political Theory of Posses-*

sive Individualism: Hobbes to Locke (New York: Oxford Univ. Press, 1962), especially Chapter V.

2.   Joseph A. Schumpeter, *Capitalism, Socialism and Democracy,* Part II.

3.   Harvard University, *The President's Report: 1977–1978,* pp. 8–9.

4.   Alexis de Tocqueville, *Democracy in America,* Part II, Book IV, Chapter VI.

5.   Taken from an unpublished lecture, "Business and the Public Policy Process," by Irving S. Shapiro, Chairman and Chief Executive Officer, E. I. du Pont de Nemours and Company, at the Symposium on Business and Government, Harvard University, May 9, 1979.

6.   Phyllis S. McGrath, *Redefining Corporate-Federal Relations* (New York: The Conference Board, 1979), p. 2.

7.   Seymour Martin Lipset and William Schneider, *The Evaluation of Basic American Institutions with Special Reference to Business,* 1979, (Executive Summary, p. 12).

8.   Melvin M. Knight, *Introduction to Modern Economic History* (Berkeley, California: California Book Co., 1940), p. 189.

3

Strategies for the Future

Pᴀᴇssuʀᴇs and dislocation of the kind confronting the
modern enterprise economic order are not easily met.
The urge to promote straightforward, uni-dimensional
policy options or political slogans is great, particularly
among leaders of government. But from all that has been
considered in this discussion, it is evident that our current dilemma will not avail itself of easy solution. To use
a military analogy, the political and business leadership
of the West has frequently been tempted to look for a
battlefield upon which a definitive testing of opposing
forces could be fought. What is needed, however, is not a
definitive battle, but a multi-tiered strategy on the part of
business by which all the social, political, and economic
elements that are potential support in a protracted conflict can be mobilized.

The concluding part in this brief essay will serve to
present several strategies that may help to build a firm
base for the enterprise system in the decades ahead and
thus increase the likelihood of a stable future for the dem-

ocratic and constitutional values by which we live. No single idea, or set of ideas, can define the future, but it is hoped that the thoughts provided here will enhance the actions of many of those whose efforts are essential to the establishment of a new foundation for the future.

Strategic Building Blocks

An integrated approach to strategy issues means identifying and responding to key conceptual areas. A successful strategy design for influencing the future will have the following criteria:

- it will strengthen the *social institutions* on which the enterprise system is based
- it will enhance the *management structure* of the large business corporation
- it will reorient *business-government relations* in a positive direction
- it will expand the opportunities for both *domestic* and *global acceptance* of enterprise methods.

This sweeping mandate for a plan of action reflects the extent to which economic success in our age is interconnected with social, political, and cultural change. The large business corporation, as an integral part of a new order—and perhaps the most influential, at a time when the nation-state concept continues to wane as a viable organizational context for solving our global problems—should assume all the dimensions of other major unifying social institutions. The business corporation, in the fullest realization of its potential, should be a microcosm of the larger society. Through its diverse but interrelated activities, it therefore should be a mirror and respond to the wide range of activities that contribute to and sustain the greater society.

Public government, on the other hand, is already coex-

61

tensive with the whole society; through its seemingly inexorable growth, the state has entered into and helped define the pressing problems of every aspect of social life. In an earlier era, the Catholic Church once performed a similar task and functioned as a social microcosm. The large business corporation, with enlightened leadership, can also transform itself in a manner that will permit this instrument of economic progress to help shape the society—and, by extension, the world order—in its fundamental dimensions.

And because the business corporation is primarily a means for productively organizing economic resources, its promise as a formative force in a world where low productivity coexists with high levels of interdependence and high social differentiation is virtually unlimited.

A revised agenda for any one aspect of business activity in our world has limited utility unless it is responsive to the realities of other aspects as well. This requires a new way of thinking, one that is as holistic and interdisciplinary as the problems business leadership confronts. The Chief Executive Officer in our day must know how to mix political philosophy, social theory, the science of governmental and international affairs, and humanistic pursuits (education, the arts, and other cultural endeavors) to enhance his firm's survival potential and assure its long-term profitability.

The term by which we traditionally have conveyed a sense of this enriched blend of political, economic, and social skills is "statecraft." It is a reflection of the speed at which our society is evolving that our conceptual vocabulary has as yet no equivalent in private business activity for this government-oriented term. The strategies presented below are aimed at the development of "business statesmanship"—a quality of business leadership fulfilling the goals just indicated.

Self-Regulation

Popular sentiment in support of government regulation of industry is a measure of the decline of confidence in the private sector generally. This support is highest among the highly-educated and professionally-oriented population, those for whom the merits of the private sector would presumably be most evident. Even among the politically conservative, surveys show, regulation has a substantial body of support: the only groups that showed a preference for the removal of governmental regulation in a 1975 poll were the uneducated and poverty-level income segment of our population, and those over the age of 65.[1] Thus, the most active and aware social elements are generally convinced that government regulation is a necessary component of our economic order.

In the present context, however, the societal implications of this trend are of greatest importance. How can the reliance on governmental regulatory mechanisms be reduced? To what extent can public convictions about the necessity for governmental interference be challenged in those areas that are detrimental to the general well-being and how can a conversion of public attitudes be facilitated?

Thus, for example, it is surely the case that the public is under-educated in the appreciation of the cost versus benefit approach, which must be employed in computing whether any given additional regulation of business— whether in the environmental or other area of concern— is worthwhile. Every time a regulatory agency sets a new standard, it is all too often applauded by a consuming public that does not appreciate that the benefits to be realized will have to be paid for by itself, as the extra costs will be passed along to them. That is not to say that any particular governmental requirement should be dispensed with as being too expensive, but rather that business should consider making the consuming public aware of what any such additional governmental requirement will cost in relation to the degree of the benefit, so that the consuming public can make an intelligent assessment.

The fundamental issue is the level of public confidence in private initiative as a social force. Clearly, if private economic activities had a flawless record of meeting social needs, there would certainly be less, and perhaps no, pro-government regulation sentiment at all. It may prove most effective for the business community to treat the issue of regulation as a challenge to be met on its own terms: that is to say, it may be necessary for large firms and their supporters to assume a self-imposed regulatory role. By taking the regulatory issue as an organizational challenge, the business community would be able to demonstrate to the society at large that private solutions to this matter are preferable to dependence on government.

Clearly, the creation of some sort of regulatory mechanism within the business community would require the most careful study and development before its establishment. The concept requires a reorientation on so many existing patterns, associations, and mental predispositions that careful sorting out of the ramifications of such activity on all levels would be essential. As a starting point, it would be useful to look at the activities of the many private organizations that oversee the activities of various professional groups. The American Bar Association, for example, promulgates a Code of Conduct, which can be adopted by the court supervising the bar of each state. The Watergate revelations prompted inquiry into the control over ethical standards for lawyers, but at no point was serious consideration given to removing the Bar Association's powers to give guidance to the profession.

In such professional organizations, internal "quality controls" of a self-imposed nature keep questions about the professions' conduct out of the government purview except when serious criminal violations are involved. It is not that these self-regulatory groups *preempt* the responsibilities of the law enforcement, judicial, or regulatory agencies of government; they simply *curtail the necessity* for governmental involvement through preventive action on an ongoing basis.

A Council of Industries

An analogous structure for the business community would provide a means by which much of the regulatory activity carried on in governmental bureaucracies could be performed within structures created by the business community itself. The rules and regulations by which various businesses should conduct their affairs would be developed in this setting, and enforcement procedures would be developed commensurate with the role and definition of this suggested Council of Industries.

Perhaps the organization of such a Council would include a government representative. The elaboration of this self-regulatory body would permit the transfer of many activities from the public sector and would permit an actual reduction in the number of employees on the public payroll who are involved in regulatory activities. In order to win public confidence for this shift, the mandate of an oversight agency or Presidential representative would have to be both broad and deep. But the prospect of reducing the tax burden, eliminating red tape, and creating a more efficient means for carrying out necessary regulatory supervision would give the creation of such a Council wide potential support.

Loud protests would no doubt emanate from those in government whose bureaucratic fiefdoms would be reduced—such is the nature of governmental politics, and it represents a prime force behind the ever-increasing size of government. But such controversy would be educational and healthy for the business-government dialogue in general: it would demonstrate the willingness of business to cooperate in social responsibilities and put the question of basic reorientation of the business-government relationship on the social agenda in a manner that reflected positively on the business community.

As stated above, a far-reaching proposal such as this would require careful analysis and wide-ranging discussion among leaders of the many communities—business, educational, scientific, financial—whose activities within the private sector would presumably be affected in important ways by this change. Responsible voices within the government would also be a valuable source of insight on this matter.

Business Intelligence

All large institutions have means for gathering, organizing, and evaluating information regarding activity outside their immediate or internal operations that may affect their future welfare. This is as true of not-for-profit institutions, such as universities or hospitals, as it is for profit-making entities. Fulfillment of institutional objectives requires rational decision making, and rationality requires an accurate perception of external reality. The only way to know if decisions are valid is to assure that they are based on the best possible information.

In an earlier era, military operations in which huge armies met in battle represented the largest logistical challenge to human organizational talents. Information-gathering began to take on formal characteristics in that environment, since the fate of an empire might hinge upon how skillfully its troops were deployed. Secret agents, communicating from behind enemy lines, transmitted scraps of data on troop movements or other signs of military activity that were assembled and given meaning in military headquarters. This activity came to be known as "intelligence," since it performed for the military the same function that the human mind and sense organs do for an individual.

Unfortunately, the military origins of intelligence operations have given the concept some negative associations in the popular mind. Intelligence work is often equated with espionage, even in conventional descriptions of business or industrial intelligence. In reality, even military intelligence and other government intelligence work have evolved in a way that has reduced covert operations to a relatively minor role. As warfare and statecraft have become more complex, so have the institutional foundations for intelligence work.

"Intelligence," as we will use the term here, is the product of the collection, evaluation, analysis, integration, and interpretation of all available information that may affect the survival and success of an institution. In enterprise-related applications, intelligence relates directly to the profitability of the business corporation, since survival is inextricably linked to profitability.

Well-interpreted information, provided by a properly

designed intelligence function, can be immediately significant in the planning of corporate policy in all of its fields of operation. The kinds of information that a business requires are as diverse as the range of its interests and activities, both present and future; a corporate intelligence function, therefore, must be molded to fit the perspective of those who can most accurately assess all the informational dimensions of the firm's involvements. Invariably, this is the responsibility of the top echelon of executive leadership. Stated in both operational and organizational terms, the intelligence function must be designed to serve as an aid to the Chief Executive Officer in the execution of his wide-ranging responsibilities.

Large businesses process a great deal of information in the course of their daily operations. Marketing research is a form of intelligence; public affairs is another form. Government relations also provide intelligence. Moving up the organizational chart, each level of managerial responsibility provides its superiors with information that —it is hoped—permits sound and relevant policy decisions. As discussed in a previous section, the actual utilization of information can be enhanced within the corporate infrastructure if employees are encouraged to share their perceptions and knowledge in company-provided settings. Efficient use of informational resources in the pursuit of economic goals is a valuable precept; intelligence functions more broadly conceived, however, take the informational process a step further in terms of conceptual depth. That is to say, it is important for a firm, facing the range of challenges that the modern era presents, to ask fundamental questions concerning *what kind* of information it is using, as well as *how well* it is using what it has. How information is brought together is a defining characteristic of a corporate intelligence function.

Global Intelligence

The collapse of the Iranian government in early 1979 is a good example of the problems that corporate intelligence must surmount. Iran was the second largest foreign supplier of U.S. oil; it was the primary U.S. ally in the Middle East, with the most advanced and well-equipped military force in the region. Its geographic locale made it the strategic guardian over the Straits of Hormuz, the narrow passage through which, according to the most recent estimates, over 50 percent of the world oil trade must pass.[2]

Yet according to published reports from reliable sources, U.S. military intelligence and the Central Intelligence Agency were completely unaware of the real threat to the Shah's rule. Five months before the Shah fled to Cairo, CIA reports gave his regime a clean bill of health. Even in the heat of the social unrest that led up to his decision to leave, the intelligence community was unable to make an accurate assessment of the situation. University professors went to Teheran and came back telling the U.S. government that the Shah had no chance of survival; George Ball, the brilliant former Under-Secretary of State—now an investment banker—and a prime example of a "business statesman," wrote a report for the White House after close review of the situation, urging U.S. support for a transfer of power within Iran long before the abortive Bakhtiar regime was created. Bakhtiar represented the politically moderate pro-Western interests, but was swept away by the Ayatollah's return.

Clearly, the Iranian situation was not unobserved by U.S. intelligence for the months and years preceding the upheaval: Iran was much too important strategically to be ignored. Furthermore, it was not some inscrutable Persian mystery. Israeli intelligence must have had an accurate reading, since Israel gradually shifted its oil contracts from Iran to Mexico and Nigeria over the year preceding the revolt. Citibank presumably had a clear private perception, for it decreased its holdings in an Iranian bank decisively during the same period.

U.S. intelligence failed in Iran because it was focused on the wrong information sources. It has been said that during the Shah's regime, U.S. intelligence avoided contact with Iranian students (who formed a major component of the opposition to the Shah) because the Shah's government viewed these students as treasonous. The U.S. sources of information were chosen, it would appear, to conform with a desired preconception.

Some of the blame must fall on the bureaucratic structure of governmental intelligence work. A former CIA analyst on Iran sees the agency as "a typical bureaucracy and the interest is in not being wrong more than in being right. You just don't stick your neck out." He was given an adverse fitness report after being told by a superior that his reports critical of the Shah were "obviously not the United States line."[3] It should be noted, however, that U.S. businesses in Iran also were taken by surprise. Even though billions of dollars in investments were involved, the business community did not factor into their decision-making structure in Iran a method of assessing independently the political risks. In the aftermath of the debacle in Iran, CIA Director Turner acknowledged that his agency needs more social and political data in the future. For U.S. businesses as well, it is important that intelligence be understood to include all aspects of a global environment that may affect investment prospects, including social, political, or cultural trends.

Thus, the information system for a firm operating in a

global context must encompass fields of information to which the corporation has only had indirect relationships in the past. Contact with governmental intelligence agencies may be useful in some contexts, but it is essential that businesses construct their independent routes to information in order to assure that their operational decisions are based on information that is reliable. Journalists, academic researchers, retired diplomats and businessmen with ethnic ties to a particular region or country can all be useful in providing an alternative informational base. The development of reliable relationships among this broader intelligence community is a primary function of the intelligence management of a firm.

The Corporate Political Realm

International business activities have a large risk potential because of the endemic instability of global politics. This instability is in turn a reflection of the failure of our nation-state system to produce a regime of law by which business risks could be reduced.

In the political vacuum created, large multinational firms have assumed a role not dissimilar to that of national entities. While chartered by a particular state, these large institutions operate in such complex patterns and across so many borders that the maintenance of the firm's best interests takes on a dimension separate from the national priorities that a given regime—in the parent state or a host country—might provide. It might be argued, in fact, that it is logically inconceivable for international business to exist if it were to try to factor into its planning process direct representation of the national priorities of all the governments with which it has relations.

The firm's leadership, then, must operate as corporate

71

diplomats, gauging the firm's options and planning its strategy from a conceptual framework that views the firm as a political actor in its own right. Though, of course, there is no legal edifice within which the multinational firm is entitled to sovereign status, its *de facto* influence on world economic prospects makes such a method of thinking most helpful for future-oriented corporate leadership. If international business leadership is to exercise the full potential inherent in the enterprise system over the next twenty years, today's leaders must utilize political realities that accurately project future challenges.

At present, the international relations of large corporations somewhat resemble those of a nation-state. Washington relations on an ambassadorial level are not unusual for leaders of major firms, and the reception of U.S. corporate heads abroad often approaches that of high-level diplomatic settings. Underlying such corporate activity, however, must be a solid, loyal, and indefatigable staff that prepares the firm's highest envoys for all possible dimensions of interaction. Intelligence functions can orient corporate leadership dealing with foreign leaders on many issues: cultural and traditional matters; important elements of the political environment; major intellectual or ethical issues for a society; the scope of relevant financial and commercial activity.

Building an Intelligence Function

It should be clear from the preceding that a corporate intelligence function cannot be fabricated according to some standard plan or design. Some elements of business operations are more susceptible to standardization than others; intelligence is one of the least standardized, most idiosyncratic elements in the total managerial design.

Rightly understood, it is an element of the corporate governance structure. Initiated to meet executive leadership needs, the intelligence role in the firm and its place on the organizational chart will reflect senior management's best judgment as to how it can facilitate a more integrated informational flow in the firm. Some firms may choose to redesign an existing information department within the firm and change the reporting patterns of managers whose work fits the new schema; others may wish to start something totally new. A premium is put on flexibility within the intelligence function, and, in its implementation phase, it is important that executive leadership keep many options open.

In its more advanced stages, the intelligence function will assist in many dimensions of the firm's work. By providing clear foundations for executive deliberation, the intelligence function enhances the rule-making capability of the corporation in ways central to the evolution of a strong internal governance structure. In the creation of a sound basis for international business ethics— a central element for the future stability of the global business environment—the in-depth informational services of a firm's intelligence function will be key.

Outside Sources of Intelligence

A firm's intelligence function must be staffed with individuals capable of understanding the essential aspects of all relevant areas of the firm's work. Beyond that, however, they must also be capable of relating to the vast external community that gathers and interprets information vital to the firm's intelligence work. The top people in the intelligence function, then, must be able to move easily in academic, diplomatic, journalistic, and research-oriented environments; they must be able to es-

73

tablish quick rapport with a wide range of individuals and kinds of professionals; they must have a ready facility for asking questions and listening well; and they must be able to turn highly heterogeneous pieces of information into coherent reports and briefing sessions in rapid-fire order.

These skills are, of course, at a premium, and the large corporations will need to draw upon top professional schools in business, law, international affairs, and related fields to find the proper intelligence personnel. The firm's own roster may include some individuals who could meet the challenge of this kind of work, and the Staff Development strategy discussed below may provide useful insights as to how to find such people most readily.

Staff Development Strategy

One of the objectives of modern corporate leadership is cultivation of loyal and effective managers. The profile of a firm's requirements varies according to the particular needs at specific times: managerial leadership at the highest level; imagination; managerial and organizational skills; technical expertise; human relation skills; diplomatic skills; political knowledge and contacts, and others, will all be needed in blends or combinations that will, in the long run, produce a successful business enterprise. The methods that are worked out for developing a cohesive and brilliant managerial class are themselves reflective of insightful and imaginative executive managerial decision making.

There are many business executive programs in the United States, as well as in Europe. It is generally accepted, however, that those in the United States are the best. But in addition to the programs offered by the major universities and by a variety of private groups, it is important for a major business corporation to develop effective, internal executive programs. Such programs need not offer simply a different mix of business-oriented courses. Rather, they should focus on a particular company's problems; its own particular form of internal governance; its particular form of the decision-making process; its particular orientation to the problem of survival. It should attempt to show the usefulness of conceptual thinking and to differentiate between conceptual thinking and operational thinking. For the most part, graduate schools of business throughout the U.S. do not become involved with the problem of corporate governance, nor do they treat the subject of conceptual thinking successfully.

High-level personnel are accustomed to thinking in *operational terms*. This is, of course, an essential element of their performance, particularly at certain stages in their careers, and personal advancement is often unconsciously equated with the ability to demonstrate success within these established parameters. The challenge, however, is to develop a program that encourages upper-level management to think in *conceptual* terms.

An expanded view of corporate options is a key ingredient in a firm's long-term growth and profitability; such a view comes only with an increased conceptual flexibility, so that people with high-level responsibilities learn to recognize opportunities for the firm that may differ fundamentally from standard operational settings.

A magic-like ingredient must be added in order to devise a program that captures and holds the serious attention of the operationally-minded. Such a program, of course, can be designed. It would follow the general points described below.

As discussed earlier in this essay, during the last half-century, American business has become one of the most complex institutions of our rapidly evolving society. This social evolution has itself been greatly stimulated by the rapid growth and structural change of the corporation, by progress in technology, by extensive product and market diversification, and most significantly, by a growing recognition of the cultural impact of business.

The corporation, originally developed as a convenient means of marshalling capital and transacting business, has become a vigorous influence among the social institutions of our day. Profit is, and will continue to be, the major measure of the effectiveness of any business, but the goals of today's large business organizations are no longer exclusively economic. If, as Whitehead proposed, "a great society is a society in which its men of business think greatly of their function," then such men—to be prepared to handle the involved and far-ranging affairs of modern business—should see their institutions as part of a larger whole; i.e., a society within a society.

Today, more than ever before, the survival of business as an institution depends not just on the pursuit of profit, but also on nurturing the values implicit in freedom, private ownership and governance, a flexible economy, the concept of the corporation, and progress with reasonable stability—all of which have created and which help to sustain competitive business in the free world. For those who would manage the corporation, mere capability is not enough. The corporate executive must be broadly grounded in his attitudes and able to make decisions and take actions that are at once profitable and compatible with the accepted values of his society.

Equally important to an adequate conception of business and the corporation in the world today is a grasp of the new level of business activity involved in the development of multinational corporations over the past thirty years. The enormous expansion of direct investment in foreign countries by multinational corporations has united the world economically and socially to a degree never before achieved, but has, at the same time, created a whole new spectrum of problems.

As detailed in the second part, an issue that is central in a review of the role of business in society is an examination of the interface between *private* and public government, and especially of *the need to strengthen the methods and organization of private government* within the structure of the large business corporation.

Further, internal upper-level executive programs would approach the study of the business institution by examining the conceptual foundations, developed over centuries in a number of disciplines—including economics, philosophy, law, history, and the social sciences —on which the theory of business has been built. This theory has evolved over the years as business has had to face every sort of economic and social problem. An approach that focuses on these conceptual foundations of business is crucial for the businessman in today's world.

In the very near future, the most serious corporate competition for manpower will be linked directly to brain-power. The great game will be to out-think the competition at all levels, nationally and internationally. It is difficult to see how this can be done without a profound conceptual and historical framework for business. In a sense, this goal becomes the bottom line for a staff development strategy. And if this goal is realized, it will not be a matter of random luck—for "luck," in this case, must become something the executive leadership of the business community has gone to some lengths to create.

Such an internal key manpower program would be designed to enable senior executives to broaden their horizons and better prepare themselves for the increasing number and variety of considerations that now enter into the conduct of a business. Basic to such a program would be the concept that the "going concern" must frequently take new bearings if it is to keep going, and that only by such reappraisal of its environment can it affirm its course and maintain its progress.

Business Philanthropy as a Strategy

Another strategy through which the business corporation can help to assure the survival of the private enterprise system is through well-planned and socially-responsible business philanthropy.[4] It is perhaps slightly unusual to think in terms of a "strategy of philanthropy" because so much of the thinking about philanthropy in general is dominated by the notion that charitable giving can only benefit the recipient. But in business—which after all is dedicated to making a profit—philanthropy must be seen as an expense that, in some way, contributes to the survival and profitability of the company. It is only with such an understanding that business philanthropy can be successfully upheld, and thought of as a strategy.

If business philanthropy can be a proper subject of strategic thinking, then it is clear that the goals of business philanthropy must be part of the larger purposes of the business corporation. A philosophy of business philanthropy, therefore, must assume as a major premise that the purpose of a business philanthropic contribution is twofold: to benefit the recipient as well as the corporation. Specifying these goals is part of the ongoing process of creating new policies and designing the structures needed to fulfill them. The particular strategic goals that business philanthropy can serve are the following:

1.   By contributing to other institutions in the surrounding society, the business corporation helps to strengthen the society of which it is a part; by making or helping to make a better life for everyone, the corporation inevitably makes a better life for itself.

2.   Such philanthropic activity puts corporate leaders in touch with the nonbusiness sectors of the society, helps them appreciate the demands of other constituencies that affect the corporation, and thereby broadens the perceptions and bases for the decision making of corporate leaders.

3.   Philanthropic grants that support research and investigation of social, economic, and psychological factors in the society are a contribution both to the sponsoring corporation and the society as a whole, and make possible more intelligent and sensitive decisions.

4.   Philanthropic grants that support research also have the benefit of increasing the store of vital intelligence about the society, which can be extremely useful to corporate long-range planning.

5.   Finally, contributions that are beneficial to the society at large inevitably create a more positive public image for the granting corporation. While grants should not be made solely for public relations benefits, there is no point neglecting the fact that sensitively and intelligently made corporate grants can reflect added lustre on the corporate world.

But it is obvious that the most important of these goals must be long-term corporate survival. It always has been, but the constancy of this goal is deceptive because the conditions of survival are constantly changing. Philanthropic activity, like all other business activity, must in the end be defensible on survival grounds, i.e., in essence, it must serve the general business interest.

The Business Interest

Possibly there was a time when the idea of the business interest could be discussed in simple, concrete, black-and-white terms: the classic entrepreneurial proprietor who had to meet his payroll personally every Saturday afternoon had a pretty clear idea of the meaning of the interests of business and could apply them as a measuring rod for assessing the variety of possible alternative expenditures.

For a multinational corporation capable of investment and operations, as well as philanthropies, both in the United States and around the world, the "business interest" bears little similarity to the historical example just mentioned. The interests of large multinational corporations today are so many, so complex, so intertwined with general social and economic matters that affect the whole society, so tainted with the unpredictabilities of public affairs, and so characterized by inadequate knowledge and conflicting attitudes and constituencies, that their identification alone—quite apart from taking actions to further them—is an enormous task and requires the best thought of the top minds of a company.

Because so many conflicting and competing parties bear on business interests, their successful pursuit usually involves trade-offs of negative and positive factors, of gains and losses. Indeed, the pursuit of business interests is now subject to many of the same vagaries as the pursuit of national interests.

The National Interest

The national interest—like the business interest—is survival—not survival at a minimum level, but robust, ebullient survival, if possible. The nation-states of the eighteenth and nineteenth centuries were much simpler than today's behemoths, and their statesmen could easily have a clear idea of what was, or was not, in the national interest. Because of this, Castlereigh could, with some confidence, proclaim that "England has no permanent friends, only permanent interests"; that is, England did nothing out of mere sentimental attachment or moral obligation, but only out of a self-interested calculation of her own welfare. Unstated but assumed was the conviction that her welfare or interest could, in fact, be easily calculated.

Now, the interests of a great nation, like the United States or Germany or Japan, are so complex that they cannot be easily stated. Is it in the national interest to develop nuclear energy—or not? Is it in the national interest to restrict the size of the catch taken from the ocean—or not? Is it in our interest to keep illegal and poor Mexicans out of the United States—or not? In each of these matters, responsible voices disagree about where the national interest is to be found. Thus, while we may need the energy resulting from an accelerated development of nuclear power, we may also want to avoid an increase of cancer that could stem from the ever-growing supply of nuclear wastes. We want to eat fish—but not just today.

The national interest, like the business interest, is now a complex formula that must encompass all the divergent concerns of modern life, and it requires experience and judgment to balance all the relevant factors; a balance achieved one week will need adjusting two weeks later. At first, resisting communism in Vietnam seemed to be in our national interest. As the conflict went on, more and more people concluded that our efforts in Vietnam were not in our national interest.

The Connection of the Business and National Interests

Andrew Carnegie was probably the business counterpart of the Machiavellian nineteenth-century statesman of power politics. And "power economics" could be a parallel term for the limited, business-interest policies of financial giants like Carnegie. Having said this, let us underscore a fact of history: since the emergence of the profit-making business organization, the idea of the business interest has been akin to the idea of the national interest. Both the business organization and the nation-state have played interrelated roles in the formation of policies from the fifteenth and sixteenth centuries until the present.

Today, when the scope of business operations reaches throughout the world, and far into the future, decision makers must engage in long-range, space-time policy formation. Under such conditions, the old idea of narrowly conceived business interests is no longer adequate. Would that we could know in every case what will prove to be in the interests of business; would that we could procure a contemporary businessman's version of *Poor Richard's Almanac.*

Despite its failings, however, the idea of the business interest, like that of the national interest, is still of value. Corporate interest, which once extended no further than the immediate community and the next payroll, now reaches throughout the world and for a generation or more into the future. The idea of "interest" is as valid as before; it is merely more difficult to identify what it is, and especially so in the realm of philanthropy.

The Meaning of "Philanthropy"

The word philanthropy derives from the Greek words meaning "love" and "mankind." The meaning is similar to that of "charity"—the office of caring—but has a more large-scale, impersonal connotation. Charity carries the image of Christmas baskets for the poor; philanthropy that of founding a children's hospital. Charity is hardly ever met with anymore on the corporate business level, nor is alms-giving—another related but outmoded endeavor. All of these were once a form of indirect social insurance, along with gifts to local hospitals, YMCAs, schools, and disaster services like the Red Cross. Charity usually had an indirect, though palpable interest to the donor; the recipients were usually known personally to him.

However, general philanthropy has increased in importance in the United States over the years; by now, philanthropic giving totals some $26 billion per year in this country. The late John D. Rockefeller 3rd, in a 1977 address, estimated that the equivalent of another $26 billion is contributed annually to society through the voluntary services of literally millions of individuals. Rockefeller, however, acknowledged an ominous sign in the same address—namely, the shrinking financial base of this sector of society. "While everything else has been going up," he pointed out, "individual giving is running at an annual rate of some eight billion dollars less in real terms than it was in 1960."[5] It is difficult to reflect on these figures and not speculate that perhaps we are witnessing a shift in the overall value perspectives of our nation as a whole.

Business Philanthropy

Business philanthropy is but a new face of traditional beneficence, modified by the modern business corporation's impersonality, its expanded constituency, its extended scope, and the lengthened time-span within which all its calculations are made. One of the chief concerns here—as indicated earlier—is to take into account some of the differences that must be considered when business philanthropy is contemplated in the light of these newer and larger dimensions. But even when we accept the maxim that business philanthropy must be carried out in the furtherance of the business interest, its concrete meaning in policy terms is not immediately clear.

It can be assumed that philanthropy is never purely disinterested, even on the individual level; certainly not on the corporate level. There is always some interest, however indirect, that is being served by the philanthropic company, ranging from improved public relations to the subsidy of external educational programs that might otherwise require total in-house support, to occasional support programs involving only tangential and indirect and long-range benefit to the contributing company, such as programs in support of the arts.

Not only is business philanthropy rarely—if ever—disinterested, it actually is a large grant of discretionary authority from society to the directors of corporate business. Business philanthropy is in part attractive because of the fact that it is 46 percent tax-supported. Up to 5 percent of net pre-tax corporate income can be tax exempt if used for philanthropy. This means that, within this amount, nearly half of business philanthropic activities are, in effect, a delegated capacity to disburse otherwise public funds.

The potential sums involved are meaningful: by 1956, it is not generally realized, business corporations were contributing nearly half a billion dollars annually for philanthropic purposes. In 1976, total U.S. corporate philanthropy was estimated to be $1.35 billion. For the same period, total net pre-tax corporate income amounted to $147 billion. Had the entire allowable 5 percent actually been expended by American business corporations, the amount would have come to a national business philanthropic total of some $7.35 billion. The unused potential of $6 billion is a massive amount of unexpended leverage that could properly have been utilized. With sound philanthropic criteria and some rudimentary degree of coordination, it is easy to see that a vast reservoir of influence could legitimately be made available to the business community. This same argument, incidentally, was advanced some two decades ago by the late Donald David, a distinguished former Dean of the Harvard Business School and, at the time, a member of the Board of the Ford Foundation. No one with greater respect in the business community could have made the observation and the recommendation, but the communication was too advanced for the business leadership of the time and, although noticed, was obviously not acted upon.

During the early 1980s, a few senior American business executives will no doubt again try to pursue the concept that corporate philanthropy is indeed a corporate strategy. For example, Thomas A. Murphy, Chairman and Chief Executive Officer of General Motors, writing to his colleagues at the Business Roundtable in October of 1979, put the matter in these words:

> I agree that corporate philanthropy is important, and focusing more attention on the corporate role in the nonprofit sector could be helpful to business. Companies should be encouraged to give more attention to this area and, hopefully, more companies would be persuaded to contribute. However, . . . this is not simply a matter of arbitrarily establishing a percentage of earnings for allocation to the nonprofit sector. Rather, it should be to identify the needs and to respond to them in an effective and enlightened manner.

As of this writing, a number of new studies and conferences on corporate philanthropy are being planned in various parts of the United States. The real leadership of America will grasp the importance and the potential of the subject, and there is hope that the business community will not go adrift on an ocean of ambivalence.

Social Responsibility

The contemporary, socially-responsible business executive will argue that philanthropic contributions by business companies can serve both business and public purposes simultaneously. In a way, these advocates take a prudential position similar to a more conservative one, holding that the business corporation must do nothing that does not lead to profit, but the prudential advocates criticize the conservative position as taking too narrow a view of the full range of interests that bear on the survival and profitability of a business organization. These newer, more far-seeing business executives point out that when corporate capital investments are made with a view toward returns twenty to thirty years in advance, the ideas of "profit" and "business interest" take on a much more wide-ranging significance. Such executives recognize the necessity of taking actions and making investments that are designed to ensure that the general business and cultural environment in which their businesses will be operating during the next generation will be one that is favorable to the security of their general capital investments.

It is, the argument goes, to the advantage of the business organization to make contributions that produce a favorable response to the company in the public mind—making the purchase of its products not only acceptable but desirable to many, and helping to neutralize unfavorable images the company may have acquired in other respects. With the growth of consumerism and environmentalism, the public image of many companies has come to be seen in a far from favorable light; business contributions that emphasize the social responsibility of the company certainly help to improve that public image.

Likewise, contributions to local schools, to higher education, and to continuing education programs may help make educational opportunities more available to employees, help the company keep employees, and help develop the talents of employees, all of which can—and do —help a company's image.

And as mandatory retirement programs are modified, a host of phased-retirement, released time, and alternative career programs will be required, and all of these can be facilitated or assisted through philanthropic programs. But all such activities find their rationale in the general proposition referred to earlier: business philanthropy helps sustain the general social and physical environment in which the business corporation must survive. As a citizen of society—and often a rather large citizen—it is argued that the world within which business must survive is one that can be usefully shaped to a significant degree by business itself. The idea is that business can survive better in a successful and well-functioning society (or region, or community) than in one where all the social arrangements are going awry.

Beyond contributions that improve the immediate context within which business operates are those business contributions that have a largely altruistic character, i.e., payments that have only a small or a very indirect benefit to the company. Thus, a mining company in the Great Plains area makes large contributions in support of opera in New York City. Except for a little personal glory enjoyed by the president or the chairman of the company, such a contribution can do much for culture and civilization, while doing nothing *directly* advantageous for the company.

Finally, it may be useful to note a certain sense in which we can say that today's leading business corporations have, and function according to, a philosophy of history. Briefly, that philosophy is that every organization of men is established to use some of humanity's available time and energy in cooperation to achieve certain ends. In the process of becoming an organization, such groups also become subcommunities of the larger human society from which they draw spiritual and intellectual resources. The business subcommunity, like all others, owes its proper "dues" to the larger society, and this takes the form of generating a set of human and humane responses and responsibilities for the survival and the success of that source society. In this view, it is mechanical, abstract, and inhumane to treat a working community or organization as solely economic or productive, deprived of all emotion, feeling, sentiment, and social responsibility or moral obligation. Correlatively, it is vital, concrete, and humane for such an organization to contribute to the survival of the larger society from which it derives. And doing so is beneficial to the survival and profitability of the corporation.

Epilogue

The vast range of forces to which the modern corporation must be responsive is reflective of the many strains on traditional concepts of corporate thinking. As the life of the modern corporation has become both internally and externally more complex, these old concepts and the systems of explanation based on them have had to yield to concepts and systems of explanation more adequate to the new realities.

The situation is not unlike that which has developed over the last half-century in the field of sub-atomic physics. On the basis of the evidence available in the first part of this century, the atom was seen as composed of electrons, protons, and neutrons. The concepts were relatively simple and the theory erected on them neatly explained the evidence in hand. Now, after decades of intense research and the discovery of vast amounts of new evidence, the old concepts will no longer suffice; dozens of newly-defined sub-atomic particles are now postulated, and new theory has been devised to incorporate the new evidence.

In a similar manner, the theory of the corporation must steadily be revised to include consideration of the ever-new factors in its current operations as the world gropes toward a more rational order for the conduct of its affairs. Indeed, the large multinational corporation may prove to be an embryonic component of that new order. We currently see a strong centrifugal tendency in the nation-states of the world in which a wide variety of cultural subgroups are seeking an autonomous base. The failure of the nation-state structure to provide a rational basis for conflict resolution is increasingly evident, and it is possible that our world will, in the near future, witness the creation of new kinds of political, economic, and social collectivities.

At present, the large corporation must continue to utilize all available resources for the perpetuation of its essential strengths, while moving decisively to meet the criticisms leveled against it. Each of the strategies that has been outlined here is intended to move the modern corporation in one aspect or another toward a rational and integrated program that will allow it to respond favorably to whatever the future may bring.

Notes

1. Seymour Martin Lipset and William Schneider, *The Evaluation of Basic American Institutions with Special Reference to Business*, 1979, pp. 129–130.

2. R. K. Ramazani, "Security in the Persian Gulf," *Foreign Affairs*, Spring 1979 (Vol. 57, No. 4), p. 821.

3. Seymour M. Hersh, "Ex-Analyst Says CIA Rejected Warning on Shah," *New York Times*, January 7, 1979.

4. Much of the material in this section is exerpted from my chapter, "International Business Philanthropy and the National Interest," in *International Business Philanthropy* (New York: Macmillan, 1979).

5. Rockefeller, John D. 3rd, "The Third Sector," in *The Third Sector: A New Perspective on Corporate Social Responsibilities* (Duke University: October 18, 1977), p. 2.

Index

Index

Index

Self-regulation, 63–66
Shah of Iran, 16, 69, 70
Shapiro, Irving S., quoted, 54
Singapore, 17
Social responsibility, carrying out corporate, 86–88
Social security, 37
Social unrest, 27, 31
Social Worker's Party, 18, 19–20
Socialist/communist movement, 31
"Socialist internationalism," 6
Socialist parties, 3
Socialist Party U.S.A., success of, 18–20
Socialists, 5
Society
  business corporation as a microcosm of the larger, 61–62
  constant evolution of, 46
  as source, 88
Somali, 15
South Africa, 11, 15
South America, 15–16
South Korea, 17
Soviet dissidents, 7
Soviet Union, 12, 13; see also Russia
Spain, 9
  communists in, 8
Sri Lanka, 17
State
  limitations on power of, 44
  power of, 36
Straits of Hormuz, 69
Strategy
  business philanthropy as a, 78–88
  for staff development for

conceptual thinking, 74–78
Sub-Saharan Africa, 14–15

Taiwan, 17
Taxes, high, 37
Terrorism, 4
Terrorists, 12, 18
Thailand, 17
Thatcher, Margaret, 10
Third World, 12
Third World nations, xix, 14–15; see also Underdeveloped countries
  risks of conducting business in, 13–14
  risks of transfer of enterprise methodology into, 3–4
Tocqueville, Alexis de, quoted, 53–54
Turner, Stansfield, 70

Underdeveloped countries
  attractions of, for large corporations, 13–14
  conditions within, 12
United Nations, 12
United States
  relative openness of society of, 20–22
  relative quiet within, 18
  shift in political and social opinion in, 1960s, 23–25

Vietnam, 35, 81
  as a public issue, 23
Voting rights legislation, 26

War powers, granted to the executive, 43
Watergate, 25, 28, 29, 64

PROGRAM FOR STUDIES OF
THE MODERN CORPORATION
Graduate School of Business, Columbia University

PUBLICATIONS

———

FRANCIS JOSEPH AGUILAR
Scanning the Business Environment

MELVIN ANSHEN
Corporate Strategies for Social Performance

MELVIN ANSHEN, *editor*
Managing the Socially Responsible Corporation

HERMAN W. BEVIS
*Corporate Financial Reporting in a Competitive
Economy*

COURTNEY C. BROWN
Beyond the Bottom Line

COURTNEY C. BROWN
Putting the Corporate Board to Work

COURTNEY C. BROWN, *editor*
World Business: Promise and Problems

CHARLES DE HOGHTON, *editor*
The Company: Law, Structure, and Reform

RICHARD EELLS
The Corporation and the Arts

RICHARD EELLS
The Political Crisis of the Enterprise System

RICHARD EELLS, *editor*
International Business Philanthropy

RICHARD EELLS and CLARENCE WALTON, *editors*
Man in the City of the Future

JAMES C. EMERY
*Organizational Planning and Control Systems:
Theory and Technology*

ALBERT S. GLICKMAN, CLIFFORD P. HAHN, EDWIN A. FLEISHMAN, and BRENT BAXTER
Top Management Development and Succession: An Exploratory Study

NEIL H. JACOBY
Corporate Power and Social Responsibility

NEIL H. JACOBY
Multinational Oil: A Study in Industrial Dynamics

NEIL H. JACOBY, PETER NEHEMKIS, and RICHARD EELLS
Bribery and Extortion in World Business: A Study of Corporate Political Payments Abroad

JAY W. LORSCH
Product Innovation and Organization

KENNETH G. PATRICK
Perpetual Jeopardy—The Texas Gulf Sulphur Affair: A Chronicle of Achievement and Misadventure

KENNETH G. PATRICK and RICHARD EELLS
Education and the Business Dollar

IRVING PFEFFER, *editor*
The Financing of Small Business: A Current Assessment

STANLEY SALMEN
Duties of Administrators in Higher Education

GEORGE A. STEINER
Top Management Planning

GEORGE A. STEINER and WILLIAM G. RYAN
Industrial Project Management

GEORGE A. STEINER and WARREN M. CANNON, *editors*
Multinational Corporate Planning

GUS TYLER
The Political Imperative: The Corporate Character of Unions

CLARENCE WALTON and RICHARD EELLS, *editors*
The Business System: Readings in Ideas and Concepts

About the Author

RICHARD EELLS is Special Advisor to the President of Columbia University, Counselor to the Dean, Director of the Program for Studies of the Modern Corporation, an Adjunct Professor of Business at the Graduate School of Business, and a Member of the President's National Development Board. He has been at Columbia since 1961.

Before coming to Columbia University, he was Manager of Public Policy Research at the corporate headquarters of the General Electric Company in New York City. Prior to that he was for five years the Chief of the Division of Aeronautics at the Library of Congress, holding the Guggenheim Chair of Aeronautics from 1949 to 1950.

Professor Eells has been a consultant and/or advisor to many corporations, institutions, and private colleges, and a trustee of several foundations.

He received his education at Whitman College and Princeton University. He has received awards from both the Alfred P. Sloan Foundation and the Rockefeller Foundation. The first edition of *Conceptual Foundations of Business* by Professor Eells and Professor Clarence Walton received the McKinsey Foundation Academy of Management Award. He has lectured in many foreign countries and has represented Columbia University at numerous international conferences. In the summer of 1979, he was the court-appointed observer for the United States Court for Berlin.

He has been the author, co-author, or editor of eleven books, and is the series editor of 27 volumes of the Program for Studies of the Modern Corporation.

The colophon for this book as for the other books of the Program for Studies of the Modern Corporation was created by Theodore Roszak